GERMAN ARMY
HANDBOOK

JAMES LUCAS

SUTTON PUBLISHING

First published in 1998 by
Sutton Publishing Limited · Phoenix Mill
Thrupp · Stroud · Gloucestershire · GL5 2BU

This edition published in 2002

British Library Cataloguing in Publication Data
A catalogue record for this book is available from the British Library.

ISBN 0 7509 3191 4

Typeset in 10/13 pt New Baskerville.
Typesetting and origination by
Sutton Publishing Limited.
Printed in Great Britain by
J.H. Haynes & Co. Ltd, Sparkford.

CONTENTS

ACKNOWLEDGEMENTS

Among the several institutions and many friends who have contributed to the production of this book, there are two men whose help has been invaluable and to whom go my special thanks. The first of these is Gary Shaw, BSc, who carried out research on the infantry weapons, the artillery and the armoured fighting vehicles which are described in these pages. When, in the early summer of this year, I suffered a short bout of ill health, Gary volunteered his help, and without it the production of this book might have been seriously delayed. The second friend is the distinguished American author Mark Yerger, who supplied the majority of the photographs which illustrate the text. Not only did Mark make his extensive archive available to me, but his assistance on a number of technical points was invaluable. The help he gave is gratefully acknowledged.

I am also grateful to my granddaughter, Victoria, who read and checked the many drafts of this typescript. Also to Julie Robertshaw and to Colin Bruce, both of the Department of Printed Books at the Imperial War Museum, as well as to Hilary Roberts of that museum's Department of Photographs. My thanks go also to Dr Rauchensteiner of the Heeresgeschichtliches Museum in Vienna, to Vizeleutnant Eberl of the Austrian Army, and to Gill Pratt. Further thanks go to Lieutenant-Colonel George Forty, formerly Director of the Tank Museum in Bovington, to Jonathan Falconer, my publisher, and to Sheila Watson, my agent. But no expression of thanks would be complete without acknowledging the great debt I owe to my dear wife, Edeltraude, for she has been my constant support and encouragement.

James Lucas
London, 1998

BIBLIOGRAPHY & UNPUBLISHED SOURCES

Cooper, M., *The German Army, 1933–1945*, MacDonald and Janes, 1978.
Hillgruber (ed.), *Kriegstagebuch der OKW*, Bernhard and Graefe, 1963.
Keilig, *Das Deutsche Heer, 1939–1945*,
Kissel, H., *Der Deutsche Volkssturm, 1944–45*, Frankfurt-am-Main, 1962.
Klietmann, *Die Waffen-SS: Eine Dokumentation*,
Middeldorf, E., *Taktik im Russlandfeldzug*, Mittler, 1956.
Phillipi, A. and Hesse, E., *Der Feldzug gegen Sovjet Russland*, Kohlhammer, 1962.
Tessin, G., *Verbände und Truppen der Deutschen Wehrmacht und SS*, Biblio Verlag, 1975.
US Army, *German Army Handbook, 1944.*
War Office, *The German Order of Battle, 1944*

West, O.B., 'Angriff Heeresgruppe "B"', 16 December 1944.
HQ 2nd Army, 'History of Operations by 2nd Army', Bielefeld.
OKH, 'Operations Abteilung. "Barbarossa"', Chefsachen Band III.
OKH (Fremde Heere Ost), 'Handakte: Deutsche Unternehmungen', Ostfront 22 June 1941–30 August 1943.

GLOSSARY

A/A	Anti-aircraft.
Abteilung	This noun has several military meanings. In an artillery unit it was the equivalent of a battalion. In other arms of service it could mean a department, a detachment or any unit between a Company and a regiment in strength.
AFV	Armoured Fighting Vehicle.
Auftrag	A mission. In the German Army it was not usual to give a direct order but rather to outline a mission. The unit commander could then carry out the mission in the way he thought most appropriate.
Ausbildung	Training; either of an individual soldier or of a unit, as in Ausbildungsbatallion; a training battalion.
Ausführung	A model, mark or type of vehicle, as in Tiger Mk II.
Barbarossa	The German plan for the attack upon the Soviet Union in June 1941.
Case White	The German plan for the attack on Poland, 1939.
Case Yellow	The German plan for the campaign in Holland, Belgium and France, 1940.
Eisenbahnlafette	A railway mounting, usually for a heavy artillery piece.
Ersatz	A depot unit or a replacement unit.
Flak	Fliegerabwehrkanon anti-aircraft gun or anti-aircraft fire.
Luftwaffefelddivision	A division that had once been on the strength of the German Air Force but which had been converted to fight as standard infantry.
HMG	Heavy machine gun.
Horchkompanie	A wireless intercept company.
Kampfwagenkanone	A tank gun, usually meaning the vehicle's main armament, and thus a weapon of high velocity.
Leichtemaschinengewehr	Light machine-gun.
Lehrbatallion	A demonstration battalion.
LMG	Light machine gun.
Oberkommando	High Command, as in Oberkommando des Heeres (OKH) – the Army High Command, Oberkommando der Luftwaffe (OKL) – the High Command of the German Air Force, Oberkommando der Marine (OKM) – the Navy High Command and the Oberkommando der Wehrmacht (OKW) – the High Command of the Armed Forces.
PAK	Panzerabwehrkanon or anti-tank gun.
Nebelwerfer	Literally, a smoke projector, but in fact a multi-barrelled rocket projector firing high explosive projectiles.

PzKw	Panzerkampfwagen; an armoured fighting vehicle, usually a tank.
Panzerbergzug	A tank recovery platoon.
Panzerbüchese	Anti-tank rifle.
Panzergrenadier	The infantry component of a Panzer or Panzergrenadier Division.
Patrone	A cartridge or, more loosely, an artillery projectile.
Reichsarbeitsdienst/RAD	The National Labour Service in which young German men were given pre-military training and were made physically fit through hard work. During the war RAD Divisions served as infantry on the Eastern Front.
Regiment	In the German army an infantry regiment was made up of three battalions.
Rueckstossfrei	Recoilless.
Sea Lion	Aborted German invasion of the British Isles.
Seeloewe	The plan to invade the British Isles in 1940.
Schweremaschinengewehr SMG	Heavy machine-gun.
SP	Self-propelled.
SPW	Schützenpanzerwagen or armoured vehicle, in which infantry usually, Panzergrenadiers, were carried.
SS	Schützstaffel ('Protection Squad') – Nazi military organization.
Sturmkanone	An assault gun with a long barrel.
Sturmgeschütz	An assault gun with a short barrel.
Sturmregiment	An assault regiment.
Übung	A military exercise or, in the artillery, a practice shell which emitted smoke when it exploded.
Verstärkte	Usually an infantry regiment which was reinforced to the strength of a Brigade group.
Volkssturm	A civilian lêvée en masse raised towards the end of the war by the Nazi party. The battalions of the Volkssturm were activated on the orders of the senior Nazi party official in the Gau or province, i.e., the Gauleiter.
Waffen SS	A branch of the SS, a Party organization. The Waffen SS expanded into nearly forty fully armed divisions who usually fought with outstanding bravery.
Wehrkreis	A military district.
Zitadelle	The plan for the offensive at Kursk in 1943.
Zug	This noun has several meanings, including a platoon, a railway train or a tractor.

FOREWORD

This work is a handbook of the German Army which fought the Second World War from 1 September 1939 to 9 May 1945. For readers to gain the maximum benefit from this text it is important that certain things are explained and understood.

Firstly, in every army there are minor units and obscure detachments which do not fit into the standard pattern of military bodies. The German Army was no exception to that rule, but because of limitations of space, details of such military miscellania have been omitted, although passing reference will be made to them where appropriate and if necessary.

Secondly, in the course of a war which spanned more than five years, both the men who led the major formations and the units they commanded changed several times. There has to be a cut-off date in order to establish a point of reference, and I have selected the end of 1944. Formations will be described as they were at that date.

Thirdly, following on from the second point, it will be appreciated that there were advances in weapons technology, in vehicle speeds as well as in the upgunning and other improvements in the defensive protection of armoured fighting vehicles. Some of the weapons and armoured fighting vehicles (AFVs) fielded by the Germans were in use throughout the war, but others became obsolete quite early. The focus will be upon the weapons which were in service throughout the war, or upon those which entered service late in 1944.

In unit strengths, too, there were changes and alterations, both in the number of soldiers fielded as well as in the scale of weapons issued. The fast-firing weapons of 1944 made it possible for just a few soldiers armed with the newer weapons to produce the same volume of fire as that which in earlier years would have been put up by a whole platoon of men. Thus the scales of men and weapons shown will be those of late 1944. Enlarging on that point, the German Army, like all other military forces, had two strength establishments: the strength a unit *ought* to have had in men or weapons; and that which it *actually* had on active service. Those figures are known in German as the Soll (projected strength) and the Ist (actual figure). All totals shown in the charts in this book are Soll figures.

A volume about the army of his enemy was a vital tool for the commander of a friendly force, for it was essential for him to have as much information as possible on the opponent's strengths, weaknesses, weapons, tactics and morale. Of equal importance was the personality of the enemy commander. Was he aggressive, or was he defensively minded; rigid in application or pragmatic; and, very importantly, did he have flair? In military history, success in the field often came to the leader who could see 'the other side of the hill'. A handbook compiled by the intelligence branch of his own army on the enemy force played a large part in allowing him to do this.

This handbook, which is based on Allied wartime intelligence sources as well as on post-war works by German military historians, presents the German Army as it was towards the end of the war. By that time, that Army was no longer capable of initiating major campaigns such as those which it had launched against the West in 1940, against the Soviet Union in 1941, and the vast offensives of the war on the Eastern Front, but it remained a mighty weapon of war whose structure and organization are still of absorbing interest even five decades later. In the pages of this work can be seen the rise of the Panzer arm of service until it usurped the premier place formerly held by the infantry, and also how the Waffen-SS organization rose from a handful of individual regiments at the beginning of the war to become in time a rival of the standing Army. The Panzer forces of the Waffen-SS, in particular, gained for themselves such a reputation for combat efficiency on the battlefield that they were used as 'fire brigades' in every European theatre of operations.

From the statistics and details given throughout the text, the reader will become aware of the flexibility of the German Army in the matter of battlefield command and tactics – flexibility which allowed it to dominate military operations for the greater part of the Second World War.

CHAPTER ONE

INTRODUCTION

'The German Army is the German people under arms' was the proud boast which had guided and inspired the soldiers of that Army since the creation of the Empire in 1871. As a declaration of faith it was as true under Hitler as it had been under the Kaisers.

The German Army which fought the Second World War was one of three armed services. Under the unity of command policy which Hitler introduced, these were not so much individual forces as partners in a tripartite organization. The Army still considered itself *primus inter pares* ('first among equals'), but was forced to accept that it was just a partner. Later, another service would be created, adding another partner to the tripartite group: the Waffen-SS. As that organization, which was not a national but a

Senior officers of the Wehrmacht at a pre-war military parade in Berlin. From left to right: Milch (Luftwaffe), Keitel (OKW), Brauchitsch (OKH) and Raeder (Navy).

This dramatic photograph shows an infantryman throwing a stick-grenade as he repels an enemy attack on the Eastern Front.

Nazi Party body, rose in numbers and influence, so did the Army diminish.

The Army, Navy and Air Force were under the authority of the Armed Forces High Command (Oberkommando der Wehrmacht – OKW) whose component parts were the High Commands of the Army (Oberkommando des Heeres – OKH), of the Navy (Oberkommando der Marine – OKM) and of the Air Force (Oberkommando der Luftwaffe – OKL). The Waffen-SS, although under the aegis of Himmler's party organization, was also subordinate to both the OKW and OKH when its own divisions and corps were in the field.

The unified structure of the armed forces made it not only possible but very easy to transfer whole units from one service to another. In the section dealing with the 9th Mountain 'Gebirgs' Division, it will be seen that that division received reinforcements of men from the Luftwaffe's disbanded 'Boelcke' fighter squadron. In

like fashion, the depleted ranks of the 7th SS Mountain Division in Jugoslavia were filled out with drafts taken from German Navy units in the Aegean, who had previously served with another SS Gebirgs Division. There were many similar examples of cross-service postings, particularly towards the end of the war. This was a very flexible system of operating, and indeed flexibility can be seen as one of the chief characteristics of the Wehrmacht. It was that flexibility which enabled commanders conducting operations to create battle groups (Kampfgruppen) to meet any military need which might arise. The commanders knew that the rank and file would fight with as much *élan* in a hastily created Kampfgruppe as they would in their parent units. The confidence of the generals was justified because the soldiers considered themselves to be not so much Prussian infantry, Saxon engineers, Austrian Panzermen or Bavarian gunners, but rather soldiers in the common cause of service to the German Fatherland.

That they had been conscripted into the service was less important to them than the fact that in the armed forces they had the opportunity to serve Germany and, for the overwhelming majority of them, this was an opportunity which was eagerly grasped. From Napoleonic days, conscription had been the means by which the ranks of the Army's regiments had been filled, and over the course of decades the average German man no longer saw the few years spent in the Army as servitude – which had been the case in feudal days – but as an honourable duty to his Fatherland. Conscription was abolished during the period of the post-Imperial Republic of Weimar (1918–33), and was replaced by a professional force of volunteers. These were soldiers in a weak Army whose potency had been eroded by the conditions of the Treaty of Versailles. Those conditions not only forbade the Army to have tanks or heavy artillery, but also ordered the disbanding of its general staff, the Army's brain. Another Allied edict was that the Army's brawn, its soldiers, had to be reduced in number to just 100,000 men. That weakness in numbers coupled with lack of suitable weapons had forced the military leaders of Weimar Germany to rethink national strategy and to see their Army's future role as being wholly defensive. It is the measure of Hitler's success that within a few years he had eradicated the defeatist attitudes which those commanders had accepted as irrevocable for more than a decade.

Not that the Nazi Party had been alone in its efforts. Earlier than its attempts, Hans von Seeckt, the Commander-in-Chief of the Army from 1920 to 1926, sought covert ways

Field-Marshal Paul von Hindenburg (1847–1934) was the bridge between the old Army and the new. He is seen here escorted by General Hans von Seeckt, Commander-in-Chief of the German Army from 1920 to 1926.

Adolf Hitler, leader of the Nazi Party, Reichs Chancellor, Supreme Commander of the OKW and the OKH. He committed suicide in Berlin, April 1945.

military purposes. During Seeckt's period of office he created links with the Soviet Communist government, and in a secret agreement, the German Army and the embryo Luftwaffe were able to develop and practise on Soviet territory those battlefield techniques which later became known as 'Blitzkrieg'.

When Hitler and the National Socialist Party which he led came to power on 30 January 1933, the first moves were made towards fulfilling one of the main parts of the Nazi programme: 'We [the Nazi Party] demand the abolition of the mercenary army [of the Weimar republic] and its replacement by a national army of the people [one made up of conscripted soldiers]'. Hitler made good this pledge within two years and, by reintroducing conscription, convinced the German people that under him the Reich would be made strong again and its Army restored to its former place among the great military powers of Europe. With impressive speed, the Führer raised the Army from the weak Weimar force of seven infantry divisions in 1933 to a mighty body of fifty-one divisions by 1939. That total consisted mainly of infantry formations, but also included five Panzer, four Light or Motorized and three Gebirgs Divisions.

To aid the expansion of the Army which Hitler demanded, the OKW relied upon an existing nationwide military framework. The Reich was organized territorially into Military Districts (Wehrkreise or Wehrbezirke – see map opposite, each of which was an administrative body for the corps, usually two in number, which were raised in its district. Those corps contained field and depot divisions as well as replacement regiments of infantry and artillery. In peacetime, the Wehrkreis was the highest level in the military hierarchy, and the corps was the senior military body within the Wehrkreis.

Following the outbreak of war, two major levels of Army hierarchy were set up: a Field

through which the Army's potency could be increased and the restrictions of Versailles evaded. He realized that although the treaty limited the number of men who could serve in the Army, nothing had been laid down about the type of training they were to be given. From the volunteers who came forward to serve in the Army he selected the best, and set out to create from this body of hand-picked soldiers a force of leaders. To achieve this, each member of the rank and file was trained to take over the duties of the man immediately senior in rank to him, and the officers were sent to technical institutes and to universities, where they became familiar with modern techniques which could be adapted for

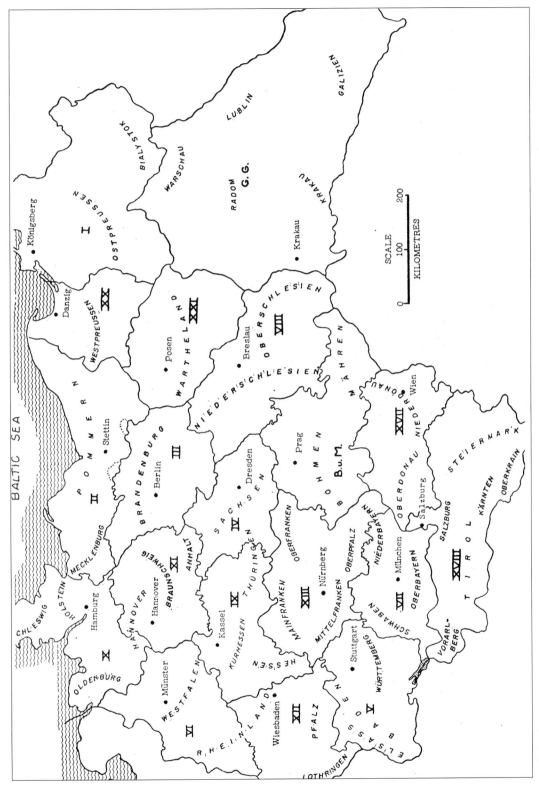

Wehrkreise.

Army, usually made up of two corps; and an Army Group, containing two Field Armies. Those major bodies had existed in peacetime, but only in embryo form. To support those major formations when they were raised for active service there were cadres of units, known as Army or Army Group Troops, which included heavy artillery, engineers, service units and similar administrative formations. Those various bodies were not on permanent attachment to any particular major formation, but lay in suspended animation until the OKW decided which Armies/Army Groups were to fight in a new war. Then, from the reservoir of support formations, the OKW would make a selection and appoint them to their new parent unit.

In the years preceding the Second World War, there were fifteen Wehrbezirke, each of which had a territorial affiliation. For example, Wehrkreis I in Königsberg controlled the I and XXVI Corps, which between them raised and administered a number of divisions.

Listed below are the Wehrkreise, showing their numbers, the territorial affiliation and the divisions (infantry unless otherwise stated) which were on establishment at the outbreak of war in September 1939.

WEHR-BEZIRK	HQ	DIVISIONS RAISED
I	Königsberg	1st, 11th and 21st
II	Stettin	12th and 32nd
III	Berlin	3rd and 23rd
IV	Dresden	4th, 14th and 24th
V	Stuttgart	5th, 25th and 35th
VI	Munster	5th, 16th and 26th
VII	Munich	7th, 27th and 1st Gebirgs Division
VIII	Breslau	8th, 18th and 28th
IX	Kassel	9th and 15th
X	Hamburg	22nd and 30th
XI	Hannover	19th and 31st
XII	Wiesbaden	33rd, 34th and 36th
XIII	Nuremberg	10th, 17th and 46th
XVII	Vienna	44th and 45th
XVIII	Salzburg	2nd and 3rd Gebirgs Divisions

At the end of the Polish campaign, two further territorial corps were added to the establishment:

XX	Danzig
XXI	Posen

Later additions to the Wehrkreise list were:

General Government	Cracow
Bohemia	Prague

It will have been noted that the list of Wehrkreise has four blank spaces: XIV, XV, XVI and XIX. These were held open for the command structure of the proposed Panzer, Motorized and Light Divisions:

XIV	Magdeburg
XV	Jena
XVI	Berlin
XIX	Vienna

Listed below are the Army Groups and the Field Armies as they were in 1944.

Army Group North	von Kuechler
Army Group Centre	von Kluge
Army Group South	von Manstein
Army Group A	von Kleist
Army Group B	Rommel
Army Group West	von Rundstedt
Army Group E	Loehr
Army Group F	von Weichs

Although each Army Group was identified by a letter or by a geographical location, it was also often given the name of its commander. In the early years of the war, Army Groups had been all-German in composition. In later years, as Germany's manpower resources diminished, major formations from one of its allies were added to an Army Group's order of battle. For example, in July 1944, Army Group Raus (later Army Group Heinrici) was made up of the 1st Panzer Army and 1st Hungarian Army, while Army Group von Weichs contained the 2nd Army, 2nd Panzer Army and 2nd Hungarian Army. Army Group Balck had the 5th Army and 3rd Hungarian Army on its establishment, and Army Group Woehler, which underwent a series of changes, had in the spring and summer of 1944, the 8th Army and 4th Romanian Army, an arrangement which changed to become the 8th Army and 2nd Hungarian, which then changed again in November 1944, when the 1st Hungarian Army replaced the 2nd.

THE FIELD ARMIES

The organization of the Field Army is shown on page 15.

When the war against Russia began in June 1941, the disposition of the Field Armies was as follows: Eastern Front – 2nd, 4th, 6th, 9th, 11th, 16th, 17th and 18th; Western Front – 1st, 7th and 15th; Balkans – 12th.

THE CORPS OF THE GERMAN ARMY

The infantry corps of the German Army, with the exception of 'Großdeutschland', 'Feldherrenhalle' and 'Afrika', carried a number between I and CI. It was usual to give the corps number in Roman numerals, but when confusion was experienced in reading numbers (for example, between XXXIX and XXXXIX, or mistaking the number L for 50 for the abbreviation L for Luftwaffe) the use of either Roman or Arabic numbers was permitted.

At the start of 1940, the number of corps had risen to 27, and in the second half of the war in the west in 1940, that number had again

Hitler and von Manstein during a visit which the Führer made to the Eastern Front in 1943. Hitler is wearing cotton wool in his ears as protection against the engine noise of the aircraft in which he was returning to Germany.

Grenadiers of the 'Großdeutschland' Division moving forward to recapture lost ground. They are crossing an area which is littered with the bodies of fallen Russian soldiers. The black stripe on the right arm of the grenadier in winter camouflage clothing was used to identify a German soldier wearing captured Russian clothing.

increased. When the German forces attacked the Soviet Union, the strength consisted of 31 corps of standard infantry, 3 Gebirgs corps, 12 motorized and the Afrika Corps.

THE ARMIES OF THE GERMAN ARMY

The mobilization plan foresaw ten Army Commands: Nos 1, 2, 3, 4, 5, 7, 8, 10, 12 and 14. Then a 9th Army was created, as were a new 2nd Army, a 4th, 6th, 7th, 12th, 16th and 18th.

At the start of the war with Russia, the Armies were disposed as follows: Eastern Front – 2nd, 4th, 6th, 9th, 11th, 16th, 17th and 18th; Western Front – 1st, 7th and 15th; Balkans – 12th; Norway – the 'Norway' Army.

As the result of the loss of the 6th Army in Stalingrad and the 5th Panzer Army in

Tunisia, a new 6th was raised on 6 March 1943, plus a new 8th and a new 10th, 14th and 19th.

At the beginning of 1944, there were the following infantry armies: in the East – 2nd, 4th, 6th, 8th, 9th, 16th, 17th, 18th and 20th, together with the 1st, 2nd, 3rd and 4th Panzer Armies (the 2nd Army was renamed the East Prussian Army); in the West – 1st, 7th, 15th and 19th; in Italy – 10th and 14th; Balkans – Panzer Army No. 2; Norway – the 'Norway' Army, later the 20th (Gebirgs) Army.

Towards the end of 1944, Panzer Group West was renamed Panzer Army No. 5, and SS Panzer Army No. 6 and SS Army No. 11 were created (the 11th SS Army was later incorporated into the Army organization, and was accordingly struck off the strength of the SS). A new 12th Army was formed around remnants of Army Group North (formerly Army Group Centre), a 21st Army out of the remnants of the 4th Army, a 24th Army out of V Reserve Corps, a 25th Army out of the staffs of the Supreme Commander Netherlands and the 'Narwa Detachment'. Out of what had been the XI Airborne Corps, the 1st Para Army was formed.

In Italy, the 'Ligurian' Army was created. This was a mixed German/Italian force.

ARMY GROUPS OF THE GERMAN ARMY

Army Groups in the context of this book were major formations which usually bore the name of their commanders and which often had a second army on their order of battle. That second army was often drawn from the armed forces of Germany's allies.

In July 1944, Army Group Raus (later Army Group Heinrici) was made up of the 1st Panzer Army and 1st Hungarian Army. In November 1944, Army Group Student had on strength the 1st Para Army and the 15th Army. In July 1942, Army Group Weichs was in charge of the 2nd Army, 2nd Hungarian Army and 2nd Panzer Army. In December 1942, Army Group Hoth controlled the 4th Panzer Army and 4th Romanian Army. During September 1942, Army Group Fretter-Pico had the 6th Army and 2nd Hungarian Army in its charge, an arrangement which was later changed to the 5th Army and 3rd Hungarian Army. In March 1945, Army Group Balck had the 6th Army and the 3rd Hungarian Army on its establishment.

Army Group Woehler had a number of orders of battle. In the spring and summer of 1944, it had the 8th Army and the 4th Romanian, an arrangement which changed during October 1944 to the 8th Army and 2nd Hungarian. A month later, the Army Group changed its composition to the 8th

Field-Marshal Friedrich Paulus (1890–1957) commanded the 6th Army, which attacked Stalingrad in the autumn of 1942, was surrounded there and destroyed in February 1943. Paulus was held as a prisoner of war in Russia until 1953, and died four years later.

Army and 1st Hungarian. In the autumn of 1942 Army Group Ruoff had the 17th Army and 3rd Romanian on its order of battle. In Italy, the Army Group Liguria was made up of that Army and the 14th Army.

THE ORGANIZATION OF THE ARMY

With the reintroduction of conscription in 1935, plans were drawn up so that the confusion which had arisen in 1914 when General Mobilization was proclaimed could be avoided. When the mobilization orders of 1914 were issued, so many men reported in the early days that their numbers swamped the Army induction process. By 1938, the

Third Reich had worked out its mobilization plans, and these were ready to be implemented. The most important was that Germany's future soldiers were to be inducted in 'waves' or annual classes: men of the same age who had acquired the same standard of pre-military training, either in the Hitler Youth or in the National Labour Service (Reichsarbeitsdienst – RAD).

In the final year of peace, the mobilization plans were gradually introduced. Among the first groups to be conscripted were men of the oldest classes, who had already completed some form of military service and whose call-up was intended to give them a refresher training course. As the result of this slow and carefully controlled conscription, the Army was built up to fighting strength, both in men and formations, with no disruption to national life. The conscription scheme ran so well that in the first years of the war it was possible for men to be discharged from the service because of their occupation or on medical grounds. It had always been an accepted practice in Imperial times that students and others who were in reserved occupations could have their call-up deferred or even cancelled. The Nazi government continued that practice, and at the end of the campaign in France in 1940, Hitler even found it possible to demobilize a number of the men in the older 'waves'. That flexible system of conscription remained unchanged until Germany suffered a series of serious defeats on both the Eastern and Western Fronts. Thereafter, not only were those men who had already been demobilized recalled to the colours, but both the lower and upper age limits to conscription were amended. In 1943, the failure of the German summer offensive at Kursk (Operation CITADEL) forced the Army onto the defensive, and the severe manpower losses which had been suffered compelled the *en bloc* transfer of Luftwaffe and Navy units into the Army and also into the SS, in order to maintain the strength of the Field Army.

These measures, stringent though they were, were not enough to cover the continuing losses, and the deteriorating situation forced Hitler to abandon earlier directives on exemptions. Even men who had been excused front-line service because they were the last sons of families or were the fathers of large families became eligible for conscription. Men who in earlier years would have been discharged on medical grounds were kept in the service and formed into battalions or even regiments of men with the same medical complaint or disability. Thus, Allied troops who invaded Normandy in June 1944 found whole formations of German soldiers with stomach complaints, and others who had hearing difficulties. Later in the war, increasingly stringent comb-outs of rear-echelon military formations and of the civil population were able to produce a limited number of men for the front line, but the shortage could not be resolved even when the Volkssturm (the Nazi Party's *lêvée en masse* of civilians) was raised late in 1944.

It had been one of the German Army's most strongly held policies that only German citizens were eligible to serve in it, but in a dramatic change of policy, it was decided late in 1942 that foreign volunteers would also be permitted to enlist. This was a move that had already begun in the Waffen-SS, an organization which, not being bound by the Army's restrictive policy, had recruited aliens as early as 1940. The extent of that SS recruiting campaign can be seen in the fact that thirty-nine Waffen-SS divisions were raised. In this context, mention must be made of the differences in nomenclature of Waffen-SS units. The SS divisional titles described three types of men: national Germans (Reichsdeutsche – those born within the 1938 borders of the Reich); ethnic

Infantry moving forward in the opening stages of the war against Russia, July 1941.

Germans (Volksdeutsche – those living in foreign countries outside the 1938 borders); and foreign volunteers.

Reichsdeutsche formations had a simple description of name and type – Jäger or Panzer. Volksdeutsche units carried the term 'Freiwillige' ('volunteer') in their titles (for example, the 7th SS Freiwillige Gebirgs Division 'Prinz Eugen'), while foreign units bore the description 'Waffen' ('weapon') in theirs. An example of this was the 13th Waffen Gebirgs Division of the SS 'Handschar' Croatian No. 1. There was an exception to that rule in the 5th SS Panzer Division 'Viking', which was made up of neither Reichsdeutsche nor Volksdeutsche, but of foreigners (Norwegians, Danes and Dutch), and did not bear the distinction 'Freiwillige'. When the Army began to recruit foreigners, it restricted itself chiefly to the Asiatic and non-Russian peoples of the Soviet Union, who were formed into infantry divisions. Later in the war, a Cossack cavalry division was raised by the Army authorities.

To some extent, the decline in the numbers of men holding the battle line could be overcome by arming the soldiers with newer weapons which had faster firing capabilities, so that the same volume of fire could be achieved using fewer soldiers. The advantage gained by equipping front-line units with those fast-firing guns was short-lived, for the Red Army's high command ordered massive increases in the weight and number of Soviet partisan attacks. To combat this uprising in the Army's rear area, whole divisions of German soldiers had to be taken from the battle line and put into action, a loss of manpower for which no faster-firing machine guns could compensate.

At this point it is necessary to explain one aspect in the wartime structure of the OKH. That force, which had been a single body in peacetime, divided upon mobilization, with one branch forming the Field Army and the second making up the Replacement Army (Ersatzheer). The tasks of the latter included training replacements for the Field Army,

Adi Strauch manning a machine gun position on the Eastern Front in the winter of 1941/2. The weapon is the MG 34 in heavy machine gun mode. The area is along the River Mius.

administration and unit documentation. This separation into field and replacement formations began at the level of regiment and extended up to that of corps. There was no such separation in the case of the largest formations: Armies or Army Groups. When hostilities commenced, the operational or fighting sections of the high command accompanied the Field Army, leaving behind in Germany the officers and the organization of the Replacement Army.

Each formation in the Field Army had its own smaller replacement unit (Ersatzeinheit). For example, an infantry regiment had as its Ersatzeinheit an infantry battalion which carried the same number as its own. That battalion gave long and thorough training to the new intakes of men, and despatched them to the field unit when replacements were called for. In addition, it was to the Ersatzeinheit that the regiment's wounded, convalescents and those discharged from hospital were returned. The system of combat formations in the Field Army and a replacement unit in Germany to train the new soldiers worked very well until a period in the war was reached when, because of the manpower shortage, the partly trained men of Ersatz units were sent out on active service to fight in anti-partisan operations.

There was another administrative division in the Field Army. The German Army made a great distinction between the combat zone (Operationsgebiet), the home area (Heimatsgebiet) and a buffer zone known as the military administrative zone (Gebiet der Kriegsverwaltung), whose alternative name was the Occupied Territory. In addition, the Operationsgebiet was itself divided into a combat zone (Gefechtsgebiet) and the Rear Area (Rückwärtiges Gebiet). To remove the burden of day-to-day administration from the senior commanders of fighting formations, the Rear Area was administered by units over whom the battle commander had little if any control. This separation of responsibilities demonstrated the clear distinction drawn by the German Army between the tasks and authority of the commander in the field and the tasks and responsibilities of the rest of the Army, particularly the Replacement Army.

CHAPTER TWO

THE COMMAND STRUCTURE

HITLER, THE OKW AND THE OKH

A nation at war must have the total support of its civil population, must ensure that its farmers can feed its people, and that its factories are able to produce the arms and machines its fighting services need. For the Second World War, the leaders of the Third Reich could be confident that they enjoyed the support of the overwhelming mass of the people, and that these would be fed. But in the matter of arms production, it was a less satisfactory situation. A nation at war must also be self-sufficient in the strategic raw

During the campaign in the west in 1940, Hitler set up an advanced OKW field headquarters. This photograph shows some of the officers of that HQ, including in the front rank three men wearing headdress. They are, from left to right, Keitel, Hitler and Jodl.

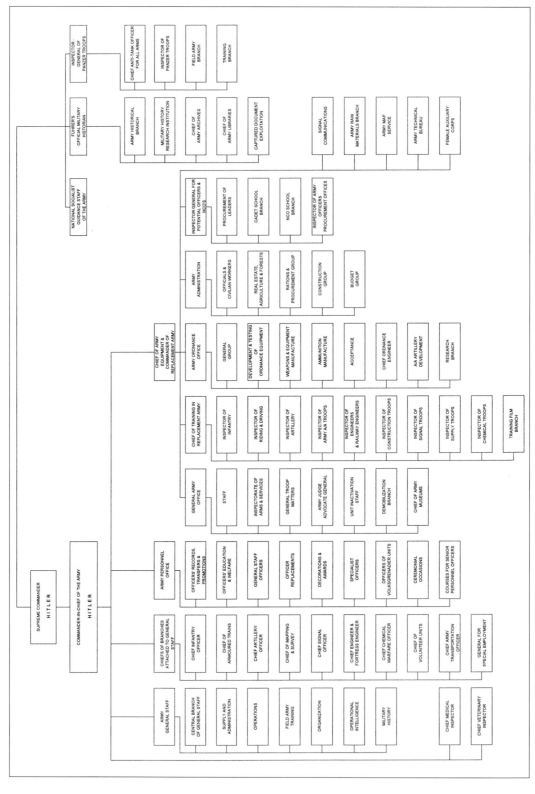

Organization of the OKW/OKH.

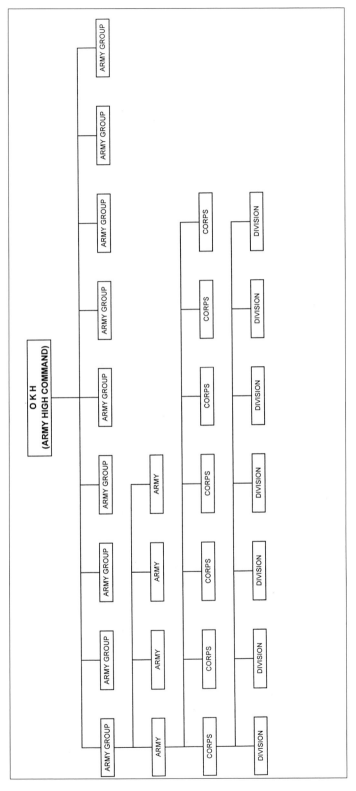

Organization of the OKH.

General Ludwig von Beck (1881–1944), Chief of the General Staff of the Army in 1935, tried to defend the service against Hitler's demands. After he was forced to resign in August 1938, Beck became the titular head of the conspirators in the 1944 bomb plot. When the attempt failed, he tried, unsuccessfully, to commit suicide, and was dragged out of his home and shot in the street.

materials essential to the prosecution of that war, or else must ensure that it will continue to receive these in an uninterrupted flow.

In pre-war years, the Third Reich was not self-sufficient, and although Hitler had demanded that Germany must achieve that status by the early 1940s, his demands could never have been met. Germany simply did not have the raw materials, nor did she have the money to buy them. Even had it possessed either, there was a political bar

which would have halted its advancement to self-sufficiency. Hitler had introduced the Führerprinzip into German life: under this, all the power of the state flowed from a single person – himself – down through the strata of lesser leaders to the common people. This principle also worked in reverse, and the orders of the lesser leaders were obeyed as if they had come from Hitler himself. Such a system of direct and tight control might have produced first-class results had all the officials been efficient or dedicated to the cause of Germany. A great number were not, and were interested only in Nazi Party matters, or their own advancement through the hierarchy of government. Many were venal and corrupt. The concept of a national war plan embracing the procurement of raw materials, the production of armaments and the intensification of agriculture, all working towards the common aim of supporting the armed forces, was an excellent one. But given venality and self-interest, it could not work, and was in fact impeded at ministerial level by Hitler's other principle, 'divide and rule', which was designed to prevent too much power being exercised by any one minister. Besides, Hitler was not capable of overseeing everything, neither was he able to make decisions quickly, and he delegated tasks to men incapable of carrying them out. The result was chaos.

Germany's strategic requirements in steel, oil and nickel, for example, were not thought through, and that lack of planning led to the Reich being compelled either to bring political pressure to bear upon its neighbours to obtain the supplies it needed, or else to resort to military invasions when diplomacy failed. Even when the flow of iron ore from Scandinavia was assured through the invasion and occupation of Norway, there was still a gap between what was required and what was mined – a shortfall made worse by the conflicting demands for priority by each of

Grave faces as the leaders of Nazi Germany and Fascist Italy discuss the failed bomb plot, Rastenburg, 1944. The group of four men in the centre are, from left to right, Hitler, Mussolini, Bormann and Keitel.

the services. The concept of a nation united and working for a common cause in every field of endeavour was sound. At the level of the armed forces, it should have been on sure ground, for it was logical that the services should be under a single command structure. But the Army, one of the main instruments of power in Germany, thought otherwise. Hitler realized that of the three services, it was the Army which was the most conservative-minded, and would be the one which would resist most strongly the demand for a unified command. He decided to smash that opposition.

In 1938, he set out to gain control of the service, and began by instigating a series of crises involving senior military commanders. Those crises removed the opponents of his policies, but also von Blomberg, an avid

Hitler supporter who held the office of Commander-in-Chief of the Army. That post Hitler intended to fill with one of his own nominees, von Brauchitsch. In order to gain the Army's most senior post, General von Brauchitsch was forced to promote closer relations with the Nazi Party, had to accept a military body (the Armed Forces High Command – OKW – to which the Army's own High Command was subordinate), and had to help bring about the retirement of certain military commanders. His compliance with Hitler's conditions cost the Army its autonomy and left it under the political control of the Nazi Party. The Führer did not need to worry about the Navy or the Luftwaffe, for both were national socialist in outlook. He was convinced that the fundamental principle upon which the than either the Navy or the Air Force. Those officers were promptly retired, and it is true to say that from the time Hitler took over command of the OKW, those officers who did rise to senior command posts were no longer dedicated to the Army *per se*, nor to its policies, but were more and more Hitler's men.

With the compliant von Brauchitsch as Head of the Army, Hitler cast about for a man to lead the OKW, and chose Wilhelm Keitel. He was an unpopular choice. In the opinion of the other military commanders, he was neither an aristocrat nor a Prussian, and was also a man to whom the traditions and outlook of the Army as an instrument of power were alien. Albert Speer wrote that Keitel was precisely the type of person the Führer needed: an ultra-loyal executive officer who was neither able nor willing to

Kurt von Zeitzler (1895–1963), Chief of Staff of the OKH September 1942–July 1944. He was dismissed from the Army in July 1944. In this picture, he is wearing colonel's insignia.

German military system should rest was unity of command, and that its application must begin at the highest military level with a single body to control the fighting services.

The changes which came about as a result of the creation of the OKW were significant. For the first time in German military history, a body stood between the Commander-in-Chief of the Army and the head of state, thus realizing the fears of many senior officers, who saw that with the setting up of the OKW, part of the prerogatives and the freedom of action of the Army Commander-in-Chief would be diminished. Those officers also argued that as their service contributed more than 80 per cent of the nation's fighting strength, it should have a greater say in the decisions of the OKW

General (later Field-Marshal) Werner von Blomberg, here seen wearing the Pour le Mérite which he won during the First World War. Forced to resign as Minister of War in 1938, he retired into obscurity, and was never recalled to duty. He died in jail in Nuremberg, where he was awaiting trial as a war criminal.

Field-Marshal Walther von Brauchitsch (1881–1948) was Supreme Commander of the OKH and directed the Army in the campaigns in Poland, Norway, western Europe, and the Balkans and Russia. Made a scapegoat after the disastrous winter campaign of 1941, Brauchitsch was dismissed by Hitler and retired into obscurity.

intervene with Hitler on behalf of the Army in which he was to rise to become a Field-Marshal. Keitel's deputy was Alfred Jodl, Chief of the Operations Staff at the OKW and probably closer to Hitler than any other general, for he briefed the Führer every day on progress in the several theatres of war. Subordinate to Jodl was Walther Warlimont, who initially accepted the concept of the OKW, but who eventually came to realize that there could be no unification because the services were divided among themselves. In the Army, for example, there stood on the one side those who supported the Army, and on the other those who believed in Hitler and the Nazi Party. Looking more deeply into the need for national unity of purpose in the military, economic, industrial and political areas, Warlimont soon realized that there was no established headquarters capable of undertaking the overall direction of the German war effort. Certainly, no national strategic plan existed. No mass production of the weapons of war had begun, and none was to exist until Speer took over armaments production late in

Hitler, von Brauchitsch (head of OKH) and Keitel (head of OKW) at a briefing conference.

Field-Marshal Wilhelm Keitel (1882–1946) was Chief of Staff at the OKW from 1938 to 1945. At the end of the war he organized the surrender of the German Armies. He was then imprisoned, tried and found guilty of war crimes, and was hanged in Nuremberg.

Colonel-General Alfred Jodl (1890–1946) was Chief of Operations in the OKW from 1939, and held that post until the end of the war. He was tried at Nuremberg on war crimes charges, found guilty and hanged.

the war. The German government had no master plan for the war economy, nor any intention of directing women to work in the armaments factories, and certainly no firm idea on how, or where, to allocate the finite material resources of the Reich. The problem of priorities was never resolved satisfactorily, and indeed, throughout the war large amounts of scarce raw materials and manpower resources were wasted on impractical projects dreamed up by Hitler and his Nazi Party comrades.

Thus the Field Army was dependent for its weapons and vehicles upon an armaments industry that was not geared to meet its demands and upon a leadership that had not planned the national economy. Perhaps

Hitler had seen no need for a vast reserve of strategic war materials because he had not anticipated that the war would be a long one. His master plan seems to have been that there would be a series of short, hard-fought campaigns, each followed by the looting of the occupied country, then the re-equipping and reorganization of the services before starting out on the next conquest. In such a scenario, vast resources of raw materials would have been a luxury. Hitler was aided in his folly by the subservience of his senior military commanders. They had seen how in pre-war years, against their professional advice, he had gained a series of successes in the political/diplomatic field without recourse to war. When war came, the generals considered him to be also a military genius, for some of his first forays in that field had proved his strategic decisions correct. Among other things, he had supported von Manstein's strategy for the campaign in France and Flanders in 1940, which had won the war in the west within weeks. Late in 1941, when the Soviet winter counter-offensive had caused the German Army to retreat. Hitler discharged von Brauchitsch and took over personal command and stabilized the wavering front line. He had now become Supreme Commander of both the OKW and OKH (see page 14).

This was all a contrast to the first years of his leadership, when he had not interfered directly in military policy, although he had advanced ideas on tactics and strategy. Then, during the war, he became more independently minded and began to plan military operations. Guderian wrote in one of his post-war works that Hitler, who had been receptive to practical considerations, became increasingly autocratic, that his ministers did their work in accordance with the guidelines he had issued to each of them individually, and that there was no longer any collective examination of major policy. Total responsibility for every aspect of the war was concentrated in the hands of Hitler, a politician to whom the Nazi Party, of which he was the Führer, was more important than the armed services. He planned offensives without understanding the significance of his actions, and refused to accept responsibility when they did not succeed. As the war situation deteriorated, so Hitler's inter-ference in the conduct of military operations increased. As we have seen, he removed von Brauchitsch from his post and then separated the OKH from the OKW and made it responsible for only the operations on the Eastern Front. He and the OKW took over

Field-Marshal Erich von Manstein (1887–1973). He commanded LVI Panzer Corps in Russia, and then Army Group A in the Crimea, before going on to lead Army Group Don. Manstein was relieved of his command in March 1944, after his forces had suffered heavy losses in the Kursk Offensive of 1943.

the planning and execution of operations for every other theatre of war. As Head of the OKH, he planned the summer offensive of 1942 which led directly to the débâcle at Stalingrad. In the planning stage of the offensive which has become known as the Battle of the Bulge, he personally supervised the laying down of roads along which the Panzer columns were to advance, and forbade any deviation from his orders.

To summarize the structure and actions of the German High Command, the OKW was an intricate hierarchy of skilled staffs with the dilettante Hitler as its supreme commander. He controlled a staff system which dealt with, among other things, strategic policy at a national level. That chain of command then flowed down from the OKW to the high commands of each of the fighting forces – in this case, to the OKH, whose most senior officer headed a general staff responsible for the detailed working of the OKW plan. It was from the supreme commander, Adolf Hitler, that a proposal would come to open a new war or to undertake a new offensive. That basic concept would be passed to the Operations Branch of the OKW, which would produce a master plan and pass it to each of the high commands of the individual services. In theory, this was an excellent arrangement, but it did not work in practice because of inter-service rivalry and because the individual heads of the armed forces cultivated personal contacts with Hitler, thereby excluding the OKW from its discussions with him.

Among the Western Allies, it was a widely held but quite erroneous belief that the German military successes were due to the smooth running of the OKW. In truth, that body was neither as smooth-running as the Allies believed nor as efficient as it ought to have been. It was riven by inter-service rivalries and personal ambitions, as well as by Hitler's indolent attitude.

On the positive side, when he took over the OKH he realized that there was duplication of duties in both high commands, and promptly altered their structures. The charts on pages 14 and 15 show the composition of both those bodies in the final years of the war. The friction between the two high commands and the Nazi Party, which had been brought about by his policy of divide and rule, was made worse when, after the failed July 1944 bomb plot, he lost all faith in his military leaders and promoted his political comrades to very senior positions in the services. For example, Himmler, Head of the SS, was given command of the Replacement Army, and party leaders at state level (Gauleiter) were given authority to overrule decisions made by senior Army commanders within their Gau (administrative district). Towards the end of the war, a national *lêvée en masse*, the

Volkssturm, was organized and carried out without the Army being involved or even consulted. Hitler had managed to reduce the OKW to being his military office, and its authority was limited to co-ordinating the plans he had ordered and carrying out his wishes without question. That subservience conflicted with the long-established Army concept whereby its staff officers had a duty to raise objections to any order which they thought to be militarily unsound. Worse was to come. Eventually, any objection to a Führer Order was seen by him at best as mutiny and at worst as treason. This was a viewpoint shared by both Keitel and Jodl, right up to the end of the war. Thus both the OKW and the OKH became rubber stamps for Hitler's orders, and the general staff structure, which had been built up over a period of a century and a half, was shattered within a handful of years.

That statement begs the question: how was it that the German Army fought for so long and so aggressively that until December 1944 (within six months of the end of the war) it was still a potent force able to surprise the Allies and to gain victories both at tactical and strategic level?

The answer, quite simply, is that at intermediate and junior command levels, its officers had been trained in the pre-war years. In the Seeckt era, the rank and file had been trained to take over the posts of their immediate superiors. The officers who in those days had undergone staff training when they were subalterns or junior field officers were able to train and to instil general staff attitudes into the men who succeeded them. Thus there was always a broad band of highly trained staff officers whose skills and abilities permeated the whole system. That the German Army was able to work so well until the end of the war was in no way thanks to the OKW. Rather, it worked *despite* the efforts of that body.

The early days in Russia. A mounted officer rides at the head of his unit as it advances into the vastness of the Soviet Union, 1941.

DOCTRINE

For many years before, during and after the war, it was a widespread belief among the Allies that the German soldier was a rigid-minded clod, cowed by fear of the Gestapo or the SS, and conditioned to blind obedience in every aspect of military activity. Those who fought against him in that war found that he was neither an unthinking automaton nor a crazed fanatic, but rather a skilful opponent who had been taught to use his initiative and who fought for his country without the need for terror to motivate him.

It has been mentioned earlier that training was the key element in German military preparation for war, and I make no excuse for repeating it, for it was of paramount importance in the military situation. Von Gneisenau, a Prussian military theorist, introduced the principle into the Prussian Army that an 'intention' should replace a direct order, and that the 'intention' had to be phrased in a completely clear and understandable manner. It was also to be framed in such a way as to leave room for personal initiative and freedom of action. His philosophy on the way a mission should be carried out was expanded by the older von Moltke. He realized that the practical application of Gneisenau's doctrine would require that commanders at every level be rigorously and specially trained so that they could carry out the task which they had been set. Von Seeckt, who commanded the Army in the years of the Weimar Republic, made it a rule that each soldier was to be trained so that he

23

General Johannes von Blaskowitz (1884–1946) commanded an Army in Poland and in the war with Russia. He then went on to command an Army Group in the Netherlands. Blaskowitz committed suicide before he could be sentenced by the Allies as a war criminal.

Field-Marshal Fedor von Bock (1880–1945) held a senior command post in the campaigns in Poland, France and Russia. He was dismissed by Hitler in 1941, and was killed in an air raid at the end of the war.

could take over the duties of his immediate superior. As a result of the training officers had been given, particularly those in the general staff, they were able to evaluate a situation and to issue clear and concise orders. All officers underwent continuous training, being rotated between field commands and staff positions to ensure that they did not lose contact with the front-line soldiers, and so that they gained a theoretical and practical mastery of the problems they would one day have to face.

Training of that intensity and depth enabled a commander to evaluate a problem and to arrive at a consensus of opinion as to how a mission was to be carried out. Thereby, on the battlefield there was flexibility in action because all ranks were aware of the intention of the mission. When Allied and German soldiers clashed in battle, in place of the rigid-minded German automaton of popular imagination, the Allies found they were fighting against an enemy which had been trained to think a mission through, to bring it forward and to exploit its potential so as to gain a success.

This was the essence of the Auftragstaktik (the formulation of a mission and a clear emphasis on the result to be gained) in place of the Befehlstaktik (an uncompromising order). The Auftragstaktik forced comm- anders to make decisions more or less on their own initiative. They gained experience and confidence by being required to act in that way. Through their training, and as a result of military manoeuvres conducted at every level of command, officers learned to issue only the most essential orders for the execution of a given task. The commander of a mission was thus free to choose the weapons he would employ and to decide upon the tactics to be used.

A comparison between the flexible German Auftragstaktik and the complicated American Befehlstaktik method of issuing detailed orders can be seen when one considers the landing at Anzio in 1944. The American commander was ordered to land and to defend himself against German counter-attacks. The landing forces found no opposition to challenge them, but nevertheless halted and waited until, in time, they were counter-attacked. A German commander in such a situation would have exploited the enemy's weaknesses and would have pushed on towards Rome. It was von Moltke who advanced the axiom that no battle plan survived the first encounter. To overcome the imponderables of the battlefield, the commander was trained to be adaptable and to evaluate each problem as it arose.

As a result of that training, when the German Army was forced onto the defensive, as it was after 1943, it switched swiftly from the creation of Schwerpunkte (strongholds) in an attack situation to the creation of Schwerpunkte in defence. It was to those Schwerpunkte that Panzer divisions could be moved to bolster the defence and through which the enemy could still be made subject to the German Army's will, even though that enemy had greater material resources. The success of the defensive Schwerpunkt tactic, as for that in the attack, depended in most cases upon the ability of the staff and the combat efficiency of the troops – all based on long and intensive training.

CHAPTER THREE

THE INFANTRY

In the German Army, this arm of service was made up of heavy infantry, light (Schützen) units, security (Sicherungs) or police detachments, as well as of the various types of Jäger formation. Also considered as part of the infantry arm of service were the para-military frontier protection detachments, the fortress formations and foreign volunteers, particularly the eastern peoples of the Soviet Union.

The standard heavy infantry divisions were of the pattern common to every national army, while those units which were considered in Germany to be light infantry would have been known in the British Army as rifle regiments, and the Jäger formations could be equated to the British light infantry. Although in the British service the differences in unit organization and battlefield role between the several types of infantry had long since been phased out, in the German Army those differences were retained because each type of infantry grouping was seen as having its specific role to play on the battlefield, and its establishment was tailored to enable it to carry out that role.

The infantry of the German Army had always been considered the paramount arm of service, and had earned for itself the title 'Queen of Weapons'. Certainly, of all the fighting services it contained the greatest number of men, and its combat ability had been the means through which Germany's earlier battles and wars had been won. Reibert's *Der Dienst Unterricht im Heer*, the

This drawing by Georg Slytermann shows a Gefreiter of the Army wearing battle order. In his waist belt he carries a stick hand grenade, the shaft of which is behind his rifle ammunition pouches. On his back are the mess tins, and below them a shelter half which constituted his 'Sturmgepäck' or battle order. Over his shoulders pass the pair of wide straps to which his equipment is attached. On his left hip is the combined bayonet and entrenching tool, and behind this the water bottle with drinking cap. The gas mask in its corrugated case can be seen at his back.

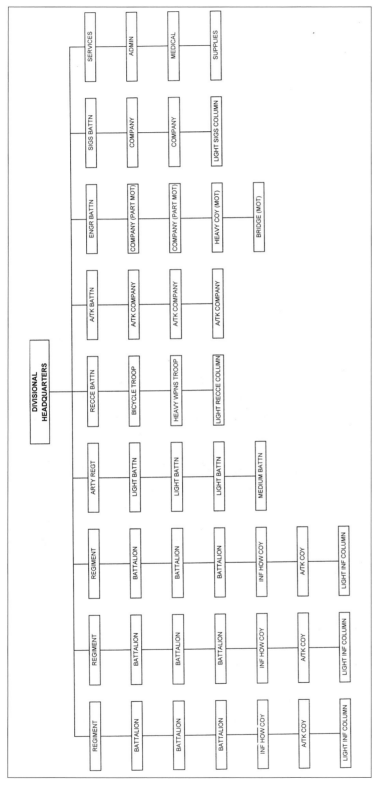

Infantry Division, Standard Pattern.

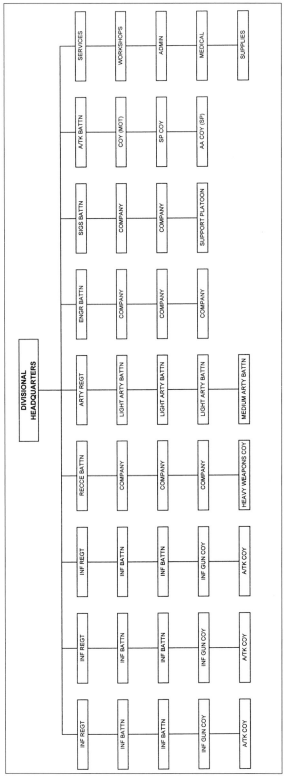

Infantry Division, 1944 Pattern.

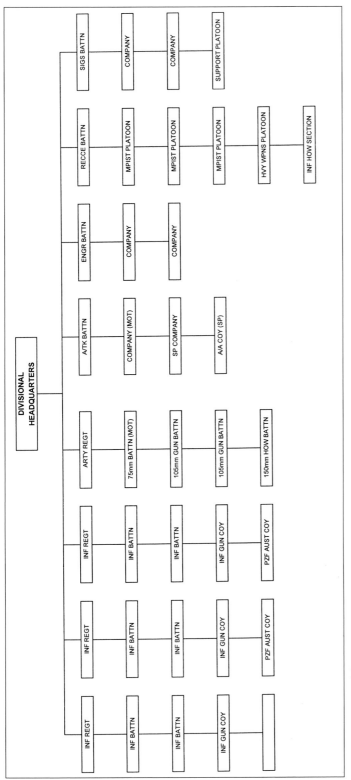

Volksgrenadier Division.

German Army handbook, stated: 'The infantry, supported by the other arms of service, decides the outcome of a battle by seizing and holding the enemy's positions. Its fighting ability enables it to close with the enemy and to destroy him.' Although the victories of the infantry were gained with the support of the cavalry and the artillery, those arms of service were held to be mere ancillaries. Only the infantry was able to defeat the enemy on the field of battle and go on to hold the ground that had been won, for the factor which decided victory or defeat in a battle was which side was left in possession of the contested ground.

According to Reibert:

The infantry company is the lowest unit in the Army's chain of command which carries a distinctive name because of the weapon it uses, i.e. Machine Gun Company. Three rifle companies, one machine gun company, a signals detachment and an HQ group make up a battalion, whose commander is a field officer. Three battalions, an infantry gun company, an anti-tank company, a signals platoon and a cavalry reconnaissance troop form a regiment . . .

This was, of course, the most basic organization, and one which underwent change and amendment during the course of the war.

Above the level of the regiment were the infantry divisions, and these were the true foundations of the Army's hierarchy. During the Second World War, the German Army fielded more than 700 of them. That great infantry mass was made up of the types of divisions described above – line and Jäger. Divisions were grouped into manageable units, known as corps, which were usually but not invariably composed of just two divisions

of the same arm of service. There were occasions when a corps consisted of just a single division or, conversely, when it was made up of three or more. Above the level of a corps came that of an Army, usually a grouping of two corps, and the most senior level of military formation above that of Army was the combination of several armies into an army group.

THE INFANTRY DIVISIONS

The infantry divisions which formed the German Army's battle line during the Second World War were numbered serially from 1 to 719. However, that neat arrangement was complicated by the inclusion of a number of divisions which bore a name instead of a number, by deliberate gaps left in the sequence of numbers, and by other types of infantry units which had their own numbering system. Finally, the political move whereby certain divisions were renamed was introduced late in the war, when those selected were retitled Volksgrenadier. They were given that description because the Nazi Party believed that bestowing so distinctive a name would imbue the soldiers of that division to fight with revolutionary fervour.

The battle line of German divisions numbered well over 700 formations, and lack of space makes it impossible to detail them all, but I have given a brief description of the first fifty divisions of the infantry line. In addition, there are two formations which were unusual, and that pair I have selected to represent the many which space compels me to omit. Considered by both the OKW and OKH as coming within the compass of the infantry arm of service were the Luftwaffe's paratroop (Fallschirmjäger) formations and the infantry divisions of the Waffen-SS. Although neither of that pair was on the establishment of the Army, both are included because they fought as ground troops under Army command.

The battle line thus included the standard infantry divisions, those which were given a name but no number, and the four divisions raised by the Reichsarbeitsdienst, which then placed them at the Army's disposal. The Jäger and the Gebirgsjäger formations were outside the numbering system of the standard divisions, as were the airborne and the SS formations.

In the last year of the war, the OKW and OKH finally agreed that aliens might serve in the Army. Consequently, infantry formations were raised from the ethnic peoples of Armenia, Georgia, North Caucasus and Turkestan – all countries which had been conquered by the Germans during their 1942 summer campaign. In contrast to what had been the Army's rigid policy of excluding foreigners, the SS had accepted all those who volunteered for service with its regiments from the early war years.

As stated in Chapter One, the soldiers of the German Army were conscripted in 'waves' or 'classes' of men. The infantry divisions which were numbered 1–36 and 44–46 were the first wave, and therefore regular divisions. The second wave was made up of divisions numbered 50–100, the third wave 200–250, and the fourth wave 251–300. The divisional series 501–600 was left unfilled so that the vacant numbers could be given to newly raised formations. Late in the war, those vacant numbers were given to the Volksgrenadier formations. The wave of divisions numbered above 700 was the last to be raised. The 999th Penal Division was an exceptional one, and also concluded the infantry divisional numbering system.

The line infantry divisions were numbered, with gaps, as follows: 1, 3–12, 14–19, 21–8, 30–6, 38, 39, 41, 44–50, 52, 56–65, 68–89, 91–6, 98, 102, 106, 110–13, 121–3, 125, 129, 131, 132, 134, 137, 148, 153–6, 159–64,

166–70, 176, 180–3, 189, 190, 196–9, 203, 205–19, 221, 223, 225–8, 230–2, 237, 239, 240, 242–6, 249, 250 (Spanish), 251–8, 260, 262–82, 286, 290–9, 301–6, 309, 311, 319–21, 323–40, 343, 344, 346–9, 351–3, 355–9, 361–5, 367, 369 (Croatian), 370–2, 373 (Croatian), 376, 377, 383–7, 389, 392 (Croatian), 393, 395, 399, 416, 462, 521, 526, 554–7, 600 (Russian), 702–4 and 707–19.

The following divisions carried a title or name: Bohemia, Breslau, Berlin, Demba, Döllersheim, Döberitz, Dresden, Danube, Ferdinand von Schill, Generalgovernment, Grafenwöhr, Groß Born, Guestrov, Hamburg, Hannover, Jütland, Kurland, Mielau, Milovitz, Münsingen, Moravia, Neuhammer, East Prussia, Silesia, Seeland, Scharnhorst, Ulrich von Hutten, Wahn, Wildflecken.

The RAD divisions also carried names. These were: Ernst Moritz Arndt, Friedrich Ludwig Jahn, Schlageter and Theodor Koerner.

The roll of infantry divisions included the Jäger (light infantry divisions), which had begun life as standard infantry, but which had then been transferred to the Jäger order of battle. These divisions were numbered: 5, 8, 28, 97, 99–101, 104, 114, 117 and 118.

From the middle years of the war, the grenadier divisions were organized as Panzergrenadier or Panzerjäger, and were therefore removed from the standard line infantry formations. They were then placed on the roll of Panzergrenadier formations, and were numbered: 6, 19, 31, 36, 44 ('Hoch und Deutschmeister'), 45, 541–53 and 558–64, the Training or Lehr Division, as well as the 1st and 2nd East Prussian Divisions.

The Volksgrenadier ('People's Grenadier') divisions, which were on the line infantry establishment, were: 6, 9, 12, 16, 18, 19, 22, 26, 31, 36, 45, 47, 62, 78 (Volkssturm Sturm Division), 79, 167, 183, 211, 212, 246, 257, 271, 272, 276, 277, 320, 326, 337, 340, 347, 349, 352, 361, 462, 541, 542, 545, 547–9, 551, 553, 558–63, 565–88 and 708.

The two infantry divisions I have chosen to represent the many are the 44th Reichsgrenadier Division and the 78th Sturm Division.

THE 44TH REICHSGRENADIER DIVISION ('HOCH UND DEUTSCHMEISTER')

It is believed that the naming of this predominantly Austrian formation the 'Hoch und Deutschmeister' was a concession by Hitler to Austrian nationalist feelings. The 44th, an undistinguished first-wave infantry formation, was raised on 1 April 1938, shortly after the annexation of Austria. No mention of the Austrian connection was made until June 1943, when the component infantry regiments of the 44th – the 131st, 132nd and 134th – took grenadier status.

The division fought in Poland in 1939 and in France in 1940 before being posted to take up occupation duties in the General Government of Poland. During the fighting on the Eastern Front, the 44th was destroyed at Stalingrad at the beginning of 1943. Re-raised on 4 May 1943, it then served in Italy and remained in the Mediterranean Theatre of Operations until it was posted to western Hungary. It fought there before being transferred to eastern Austria, where it passed into captivity at the end of the war.

When the 44th was renamed the Reichsgrenadier Division 'Hoch und Deutschmeister' in June 1943, one of its formations was given the distinction, unique in the German Army, of carrying a standard of the type formerly issued to regiments of the Imperial Austro-Hungarian Army. A description of that flag is given in Chapter Twelve.

The division's three infantry (grenadier) regiments had a combined strength of 9,180

SS grenadiers preparing to go out on an anti-partisan sweep, 1941. Note the drum magazine on the MG 34.

During the first winter in Russia, the OKH issued pamphlets on using local materials to keep warm. One method was to use branches of trees to give additional protection against the cold and snow.

all ranks. In addition there was a reconnaissance battalion with 623 men, an artillery formation of 3,172 all ranks, a pioneer battalion with 779 all ranks, an anti-tank battalion with 708 men, and a signals battalion with 476 men. The total strength of the division was 17,734 all ranks.

In the divisional armoury there were 378 light machine guns, 138 heavy machine guns, 93 mortars of 5 cm calibre, and 54 of 8 cm. Of infantry guns, there were 20 light and 6 heavy. The artillery component was 75 PAK guns of 3.7 cm calibre, 36 10.5 cm calibre light field howitzers and 12 heavy field howitzers of 15 cm calibre.

The wheeled strength of the division included 919 horse-drawn carts, 4,842 horses, 394 AFVs, 615 lorries and 527 motorcycles, 201 of which had sidecars.

THE 78TH STURM OR ASSAULT DIVISION

At the end of December 1941, the 78th Division, which had been a conventional infantry formation, was given a new description and a new role. From that date on it became the 78th Sturm Division, and was given a higher than normal establishment of weapons in order to increase the firepower of its three constituent infantry regiments, the 14th, 195th and 215th. Each had battalions made up of three infantry companies, a standard heavy weapons company plus another one equipped with infantry guns, a pioneer company, a troop of cavalry and a signals platoon.

During March and April 1943, there was an increase in strength, and the artillery establishment of each regiment was then made up of an HQ battery, three battalions of light field howitzers and a battalion of heavy field howitzers. The anti-tank battalion had two companies, each armed with heavy PAK on self-propelled (SP) artillery mountings. The heavy mortar battalion was motorized, and was made up of three companies, each fielding twelve mortars.

The SP battalion had an HQ, an HQ platoon and three SP batteries, each of ten guns. The flak battalion was composed of three batteries, and had a strength in guns of 18 light and 8 heavy 88 mm pieces.

The total of weapons in the divisional arsenal was: 616 light machine guns, 76 heavy machine guns, 94 medium mortars, 40 heavy mortars, 12 light flame-throwers, 61 heavy PAK guns, 14 light infantry guns, 6 heavy infantry guns and 24 projectors.

The assault division was created out of the former infantry division within the space of seven weeks, and in February 1943, while still incompletely raised, was put back into action to seal a gap that had been torn in the German front. Then, in June, it took part in the Kursk Offensive (Operation CITADEL) as part of Model's 9th Army, and when Army Group Centre was destroyed in the summer of 1944, the 78th was among the formations lost in that débâcle.

The division's losses in bayonet strength, and therefore firepower, were partly compensated for by a higher distribution of fast-firing automatic weapons, by the replacement of the 81 mm mortars by those of 12 cm calibre, and by the issue of hand-held rocket launchers, such as the Panzerfaust. The anti-tank unit was also equipped with the high-velocity 7.62 cm PAK, and the SP units were grouped into a brigade to give them greater flexibility.

The westwards retreat of the German Army from the middle of 1944 took the 78th into Galicia and then into Moravia, where, at the war's end, its remaining units passed into captivity.

A propaganda picture of cheerful soldiers keeping themselves warm in the first winter of the war against Russia, 1941.

A NOMINAL ROLL OF THE FIRST FIFTY DIVISIONS OF THE GERMAN INFANTRY LINE

1ST INFANTRY DIVISION

Composition

Grenadier regiments	1st, 22nd, 43rd
Artillery regiment	1st
Services	All numbered 1st

A regular Army division, raised principally in East Prussia. Fought in Poland, France and with Army Group North on the Eastern Front.

2ND INFANTRY DIVISION

Became 12th Panzer Division.

3RD INFANTRY DIVISION

Became 3rd Panzergrenadier Division.

4TH INFANTRY DIVISION

Became 14th Panzer Division.

5TH INFANTRY DIVISION

Became 5th Jäger Division.

6TH INFANTRY DIVISION

Composition

Grenadier regiments	18th, 37th, 58th
Artillery regiment	6th
Services	All numbered 6th

A division of the regular Army, raised in East Prussia and in Westphalia. Fought in the campaign in France in 1940, and with Army Group Centre on the Eastern Front. Served with distinction in the Kursk Offensive, 1943.

7TH INFANTRY DIVISION

Composition

Grenadier regiments	19th, 61st, 62nd
Artillery regiment	7th
Services	All numbered 7th

A division of the regular Army whose personnel were chiefly Bavarian. Fought in Poland in 1939, in Flanders in 1940, and on the Central Sector of the Eastern Front, where is served with distinction in the Kursk Offensive of 1943.

8TH INFANTRY DIVISION

Became 8th Jäger Division.

On the Russian Front during the operations in the summer of 1943. The advance to contact stage of the attack is led by a grenadier carrying an MG 42 across his shoulders.

9TH INFANTRY DIVISION

Composition

Grenadier regiments	36th, 57th, 116th
Artillery regiments	9th
Services	All numbered 9th

A division of the regular Army. Personnel mainly from Hessen-Nassau. Served in the French campaign of 1940, and with Army Group South on the Eastern Front, particularly in the Caucasus during 1942.

10TH INFANTRY DIVISION

Became 10th Panzergrenadier Division.

11TH INFANTRY DIVISION

Composition

Grenadier regiments	2nd, 23rd, 44th
Artillery regiment	11th
Services	All numbered 11th

A division of the regular Army. Personnel mainly from the Rhineland and from Prussia. Served in Poland, and then in Russia, firstly on the Northern Sector, and then with distinction around Lake Lagoda during the summer fighting of 1943.

12TH INFANTRY DIVISION

Composition

Grenadier regiments	27th, 48th, 89th
Artillery regiment	12th
Services	All numbered 12th

A division of the regular Army with Prussian personnel. Fought well in the campaign in Poland (1939) and in France (1940). Served on the Northern Sector of the Eastern Front from the start of the war with Russia.

13TH INFANTRY DIVISION

Became 13th Panzer Division.

14TH INFANTRY DIVISION

Became 14th Panzergrenadier Division.

15TH INFANTRY DIVISION

Composition

Grenadier regiments	81st, 88th, 106th
Artillery regiment	15th
Services	All numbered 15th

A division of the regular Army. Personnel recruited from Frankfurt and from Austria. Did not participate in the campaign in the west in 1940, but was in Russia in 1941, and served with Army Group Centre. Moved to France in 1942, it returned to the Eastern Front during March 1943.

16TH INFANTRY DIVISION

Became 16th Panzer and subsequently 16th Panzergrenadier Division.

17TH INFANTRY DIVISION

Composition

Grenadier regiments	21st, 55th, 95th
Artillery regiment	17th
Services	All numbered 17th

A division of the regular Army which recruited in Bavaria. Fought well in both Poland (1939) and the west (1940). In Russia from the first days of the war against the Soviet Union. Posted to France in 1942, the division was returned to Russia a year later, and served with Army Group South.

18TH INFANTRY DIVISION

Became 18th Panzergrenadier Division.

19TH INFANTRY DIVISION

Became 19th Panzer Division.

20TH INFANTRY DIVISION

Became 20th Panzergrenadier Division.

21ST INFANTRY DIVISION

Composition

Grenadier regiments	3rd, 24th, 45th
Artillery regiment	21st
Services	All numbered 21st

A division of the regular Army which recruited in East Prussia and in the Rhineland. Was active in the Polish campaign, and served in the war in the west. On the Eastern Front from the earliest days.

22ND INFANTRY DIVISION

Became the 22nd Air Landing Division.

23RD INFANTRY DIVISION

Composition

Regiments	68th Fusilier Regiment, 149th Grenadier Regiment
Artillery regiment	23rd
Services	All numbered 23rd

A division of the regular Army recruited from Berlin. Fought in Poland and in the west, and then on the Eastern Front from the first days. Transferred to France in 1942. Drafts were taken from 23rd Infantry Division to form 26th Panzer Division. The division was re-formed and given the number 23 before being returned to the Northern Sector of the Russian Front.

24TH INFANTRY DIVISION

Composition

Grenadier regiments	31st, 32nd, 102nd
Artillery regiment	24th
Services	All numbered 24th

A division of the regular Army raised in Saxony. Fought well in the campaign in Poland, and was active during the war in the west. Upon the invasion of the Soviet Union, the division served from the earliest days, and

In slit trenches dug on the reverse slope of a hill, grenadiers prepare to go into action. The man in the foreground is cleaning his rifle. Eastern Front, 1943.

fought with Army Group South. Very active in the Crimea, but was then transferred to the Northern Sector during the winter of 1942/3.

25TH INFANTRY DIVISION

Became 25th Panzergrenadier Division.

26TH INFANTRY DIVISION

Composition

Grenadier regiments	39th, 77th, 78th
Artillery regiment	26th
Services	All numbered 26th

A division of the regular Army. Personnel mainly from the Rhineland, but with Prussian drafts. Engaged on the Eastern Front from

A scene from life in the front line as experienced by soldiers on the Eastern Front. Note the variety of weapons and grenades on the parapet of the slit trench.

the beginning of the war with Russia, serving with Army Group Centre. Suffered severe losses in the Battle of Kursk in 1943.

27TH INFANTRY DIVISION
Became 17th Panzer Division.

28TH INFANTRY DIVISION
Became 28th Jäger Division.

29TH INFANTRY DIVISION
Became 29th Panzergrenadier Division.

30TH INFANTRY DIVISION

Composition

Grenadier regiments	6th, 26th, 46th
Artillery regiment	30th
Services	All numbered 30th

A division of the regular Army. Recruited in north Germany, chiefly Schleswig-Holstein. Fought well during the campaign in Poland and in the Low Countries. Service in the war in the east from the earliest days with Army Group North.

31ST INFANTRY DIVISION

Composition

Grenadier regiments	12th, 17th, 82nd
Artillery regiment	31st
Services	All numbered 31st

A division of the regular Army which recruited briefly in the Braunchsweig area. Engaged only partially in the Polish campaign, but was more actively involved in Belgium and France. On the Eastern Front from the opening of the

A scene common in any army in any war: an infantryman gives his comrade a light for his cigarette.

war with Russia, where it served with Army Group Centre, and fought with distinction during the Battle of Kursk in 1943.

32ND INFANTRY DIVISION

Composition

Grenadier regiments	4th, 94th, 96th
Artillery regiment	32nd
Services	All numbered 32nd, except the pioneer battalion, which was numbered 21st

A division of the regular Army with personnel from Prussia and Pomerania. Fought with great distinction in Poland and on the Western Front. Served with Army Group North from the first days of the campaign in Russia.

33RD INFANTRY DIVISION
Became 15th Panzergrenadier Division.

34TH INFANTRY DIVISION

Composition

Grenadier regiments	80th, 107th, 253rd
Artillery regiment	34th
Services	All numbered 34th

A division of the regular Army which recruited from the Rhineland. Took part in the war in the west. In Russia, it served continuously from the first days with Army Group Centre, before being moved to fight with Army Group South.

35TH INFANTRY DIVISION

Composition

Grenadier regiments	343rd, 109th, 111th
Artillery regiment	35th
Services	All numbered 35th

A division of the regular Army with personnel from Baden and Württemberg. Fought in Flanders during 1940, and then served on the Central Sector of the Eastern Front.

36TH INFANTRY DIVISION
Became 36th Panzergrenadier Division.

38TH INFANTRY DIVISION

Composition

Grenadier regiments	108th, 112th
Artillery regiment	138th
Services	All numbered 138th

Raised in Brittany during the summer of 1942. First saw service with Army Group South in Russia. Personnel included Poles and other non-German nationals. Only two infantry regiments on establishment.

44TH INFANTRY DIVISION
See above, pages 32–3.

45TH INFANTRY DIVISION

Composition
Grenadier regiments	130th, 133rd, 135th
Artillery regiment	98th
Services	Pioneer battalion: 81st; anti-tank and recce battalions: both 45th; signals battalion: 65th

A division of the regular Army, its personnel being mainly Austrian. Fought with distinction in Poland and in France. Served with Army Group Centre in Russia, where it suffered severe losses. Fought again with distinction during the Battle of Kursk.

46TH INFANTRY DIVISION

Composition
Grenadier regiments	42nd, 72nd, 97th
Artillery regiment	114th
Services	Pioneer battalion: 88th; anti-tank battalion: 52nd; recce battalion: 46th; signals battalion: 76th

A division of the regular Army which was raised towards the end of 1938. The division recruited in Bavaria and in Sudetenland. Was not actively engaged before the war with Russia, but was then very active in the Southern Sector, chiefly in the Crimea and in the Caucasus.

50TH INFANTRY DIVISION

Composition
Grenadier regiments	121st, 122nd, 123rd
Artillery regiment	150th
Services	All numbered 150th

This division was a Prussian frontier control unit, and was part of the regular Army. It served in both the Polish and the French campaigns, but then had a much more distinctive role with Army Group South, first in the Crimea and then in the Caucasus.

LIGHT INFANTRY OR JÄGER DIVISIONS

The rifle and Jäger divisions of the German Army had a smaller table of establishment than standard infantry, and consisted of only two, not three, regiments.

5TH JÄGER DIVISION
This was a regular division of the Army, when it was known as the 5th Infantry Division. It served in France during the 1940 campaign, and on the Eastern Front at the start of the war with Russia. As a consequence of the heavy losses it sustained, the division was withdrawn from the line and converted to Jäger status before returning to the Russian front.

Composition
56th and 75th Jäger Regiments

8TH JÄGER DIVISION
A regular division of the Army, this was raised as the 8th Infantry, and fought in Poland and in France before going on to Russia. There it suffered heavy losses, and was converted to become a Jäger division. The 8th then returned to the Eastern Front.

Composition
28th and 38th Jäger Regiments

28TH JÄGER DIVISION

A division of the regular Army raised as the 28th Infantry, it served in Poland, in the west and on the Eastern Front before conversion to become a Jäger division. It returned to the Eastern Front in 1942.

Composition
49th and 83rd Jäger Regiments

97TH JÄGER DIVISION

Raised in November 1940, this division served on the Eastern Front from the summer of 1941, chiefly with Army Group South.

Composition
204th and 207th Jäger Regiments

100TH JÄGER DIVISION

Created during the winter of 1940, it served on the Eastern Front. During the Battle of Stalingrad it was destroyed, but was re-raised in Jugoslavia, and remained in the Balkan Theatre of Operations.

Composition
54th and 227th Jäger Regiments

101ST JÄGER DIVISION

This formation was created in December 1940, and served on the Eastern Front, chiefly with Army Group South.

Composition
228th and 229th Jäger Regiments

104TH JÄGER DIVISION

This was raised in April 1941 as the 704th Infantry Division, before being converted to Jäger status and renumbered. It served in the Balkan Theatre of Operations.

Composition
724th and 734th Jäger Regiments

114TH JÄGER DIVISION

Created during April 1941 as the 714th Infantry Division, before it was converted to become a Jäger division in 1943, and renumbered.

Composition
721st and 741st Jäger Regiments

117TH JÄGER DIVISION

Created during April 1941 as the 717th Infantry Division, it was converted to Jäger status in April 1943, and renumbered. It served in the Balkan Theatre of Operations, chiefly in Greece.

Composition
737th and 749th Jäger Regiments

118TH JÄGER DIVISION

Raised during April 1941 as the 718th Infantry Division, it was converted to Jäger status during April 1943, and was renumbered.

Composition
738th and 750th Jäger Regiments

CHAPTER FOUR

THE MOUNTAIN RIFLES (GEBIRGSJÄGER)

INTRODUCTION

In addition to the Army's standard Jäger divisions (see Chapter Three), another main Jäger grouping was that of units on the mountain, or Gebirgs, establishment. These were outside the standard divisional numbering system, and had their own series of numbers.

In 1935, the Gebirgs arm of service consisted of only individual battalions which were then amalgamated into a brigade. Out of that formation evolved the 1st Gebirgs Division, which was followed in 1938 by the creation of two further divisions.

A list of the nine or ten mountain divisions which were raised between 1938 and 1945 can

Gebirgsjäger fighting in the Norwegian campaign of 1940, observing enemy movements and positions from a stone sangar.

Gebirgsgeneral Lanz issuing orders during the first months of the campaign in Russia, 1941.

be found on pages 44–50. The uncertainty as to how many divisions were created arises because towards the end of hostilities, two newly raised Gebirgs formations were both given the same number. In addition to the Army mountain formations, there were also Waffen-SS Gebirgs formations, and these are listed on pages 52–54.

A Gebirgs division's usual structure in terms of its armament, equipment and training was a headquarters, two rifle or Gebirgsjäger regiments, an artillery regiment and the usual divisional services, including a battalion each of signallers, reconnaissance troops, anti-tank gunners and engineers. The nominal strength of such a division was 13,056 officers and men. The divisional train was made up of strings of pack animals, which were usually distributed down to battalion level, but which could be further sub-divided to equip individual companies.

The structure of a Gebirgs division had the built-in disadvantage that it was less flexible on military operations than a standard infantry division. This arose because so much of the Gebirgs transport was made up of mule trains that there were fewer motor vehicles on establishment. The cattle strength of a Gebirgs division was 3,056 beasts, and although the use of animals proved a satisfactory arrangement in mountain warfare, it was less so when the formation was operating in open country. There, the Gebirgs division was slow-moving, because its pace was tied to that of its animals.

Gebirgsjäger towing their 3.7 cm anti-tank gun during the campaign in Norway, 1940.

A standard Jäger regiment was composed of a headquarters unit and three battalions with a total strength of 3,064 all ranks. The regimental headquarters group included a signals platoon and a battery of heavy mountain guns. A Jäger battalion fielded an HQ, three rifle companies and a machine gun company, as well as anti-tank and heavy weapons detachments. The strength of a Jäger battalion was 877 all ranks, which broke down to 147 in each rifle company, and the remainder in battalion HQ, the machine gun company and the heavy weapons company.

The artillery regiment had a strength of 2,330 officers and men, and was equipped with 24 guns of 7.5 cm calibre and 12 7.5 cm howitzers. There were also 12 howitzers of 15 cm calibre and 10 howitzers of 10.5 cm calibre. The number of anti-tank guns in Gebirgs formations was lower because it was

thought unlikely that the Jäger would be opposed by enemy armour. Also, the weapons in the divisional arsenal had a shorter range than those fielded by a standard division, because operations in the mountains took place at closer range than on flat terrain.

Very specialist groups raised during the middle years of the war to support Gebirgs divisions which were undertaking special mission; these were high alpine (Hochgebirgs) battalions. Details of these are given on page 50.

MOUNTAIN (GEBIRGS) DIVISIONS OF THE ARMY

1ST GEBIRGS DIVISION
Raised in April 1938, its original establishment included the 100th Gebirgs regiment. When mobilization was ordered, that unit, being

Pioneers of a Gebirgs Division engineer battalion during the fighting for the Metaxas Line in Greece, 1941. The box being carried by the half-standing figure is an explosive charge of the type used to destroy bunkers and pill boxes.

surplus to establishment, was posted to form a cadre around which the 5th Gebirgs Division was created. The 1st fought on every European battle front. In March 1945, shortly before the end of hostilities, it was retitled 1st Volksgebirgs Division.

Composition
98th and 99th Gebirgsjäger Regiments, 79th Gebirgs Artillery Regiment

2ND GEBIRGS DIVISION
This former unit of the Austrian Army was created on 1 April 1938. It fought in Poland,

Norway and Lappland between 1940 and 1944. Following the German Army's retreat from northern Norway at the end of 1944, the 2nd was posted to the Western Front, and at the end of the war its remnants were fighting in southern Germany.

Composition
136th and 137th Gebirgsjäger Regiments, 11th Gebirgs Artillery Regiment

3RD GEBIRGS DIVISION
The 3rd Gebirgs Division was a composite formation created out of two former Austrian

One of the bunkers of the Metaxas Line, destroyed by Gebirgsjäger during the campaign in Greece, 1941.

A headquarters company of Gebirgsjäger advancing into the Caucasus during the summer offensive of 1942.

divisions. When the Germans attacked Norway in the spring of 1940, the 3rd was chosen to spearhead the seaborne invasion to take the iron ore port of Narvik. The whole division could not be carried in one 'lift', and the men who were left behind were formed into a new Gebirgsjäger regiment: the 141st. That unit was then posted to the 6th Gebirgs Division. The 3rd fought in Poland, Norway, Finland, the Ukraine, Hungary and Slovakia. At the end of the war it was operating in Silesia.

Composition
138th and 139th Gebirgsjäger Regiments, 112th Gebirgs Artillery Regiment

4TH GEBIRGS DIVISION
The intention to raise a 4th Gebirgs Division was not proceeded with. The war in France ended so quickly that the creation of a new Gebirgs division seemed to be unnecessary. Then, on 23 October 1940, a fresh effort was made to raise the 4th, and for this two new regiments were needed. The 13th and 91st regiments were posted away from their parent infantry divisions and taken onto the strength of the 4th. The 4th served first in Jugoslavia, and was then posted to the Eastern Front, where it remained for the rest of the war.

Composition
142nd and 143rd Gebirgsjäger Regiments, 99th Gebirgs Artillery Regiment

5TH GEBIRGS DIVISION
In the autumn of 1940, the 100th Gebirgs Regiment, which had been surplus to the

In 1942 a combined group of men from two Gebirgs divisions conquered Mount Elbrus in Russia. This photograph shows the party moving off at the start of the operation, carrying the unit flags which they placed in the snow of Elbrus's summit. Adolf Hitler described it as the most 'pointless mission' in the war.

The flags which were planted in the snows of Mount Elbrus after it was climbed by Gebirgsjäger during the 1942 campaign.

establishment of 1st Gebirgs Division, was selected as the cadre for the proposed 5th Gebirgs Division. The second regiment, the 85th, was taken from the 10th Infantry division. The 5th fought in Greece, and was chosen to be the air-landing component of XI Airborne Corps for the attack upon Crete. It remained on that island on occupation duties until it was sent to the Leningrad sector of the Eastern Front in October 1941. Late in 1943, the division was sent to Italy, where it served with distinction to the end of the war.

Composition
85th and 100th Gebirgsjäger Regiments, 95th Gebirgs Artillery Regiment

6TH GEBIRGS DIVISION
This was raised on 1 June 1940, and served as part of the occupation force in France and Poland before being posted to Greece early in 1941. Later that year it was sent to Finland, and it fought around Murmansk as part of the 20th Gebirgs Army. It remained in Norway until the end of the war, and passed into British captivity.

Composition
141st and 143rd Gebirgsjäger Regiments, 118th Gebirgs Artillery Regiment

7TH GEBIRGS DIVISION
In the third week of November 1941, the 99th Light Division was changed in status and became the 7th Gebirgs Division. From April 1942, the 7th served on the establishment of the 20th Gebirgs Army in Lappland, and then moved into southern Norway, where it passed into British captivity at the end of the war.

Mountain troops preparing to cross a river during the French campaign of 1940.

Supplies to units manning positions in the high mountain peaks of Jugoslavia had to be man-portered. This photograph shows a group of porters carrying supplies.

Composition
208th and 218th Gebirgsjäger Regiments, 82nd Gebirgs Artillery Regiment

8TH GEBIRGS DIVISION

In March 1944, it was decided to create an 8th Gebirgs Division around a cadre supplied by 139th Gebirgsjäger regiment. However, it was not until February 1945 that the division was finally raised. It went into action in Italy during the last months of the war.

Composition
296th and 297th Gebirgsjäger Regiments

9TH GEBIRGS DIVISION

Towards the end of the war there must have been confusion in the OKH, because two Gebirgs divisions were raised which were allocated the number 9. Although both are shown by that number in the records of the Red Cross, neither is listed in the field post numbering system, which is the most reliable source of information on service units in the Third Reich. Nor is either 9th Division shown by that number on contemporary military situation maps. The first of the two 9th Gebirgs Divisions was 'Nord', to which the name 'K', or Kraeutler, was given. That formation, the K or 9th Gebirgs Division, was later renamed and re-designated the 140th Division zbV ('for special purposes'), and served as part of the 'Narvik' Force in Norway. The second 9th Gebirgs Division, 'East' Division, was built around Battle Group Semmering, a formation created out of a number of diverse units, such as the Mountain Artillery School in Dachstein, an SS Gebirgsjäger replacement battalion and the ground crews of the disbanded Luftwaffe fighter squadron Boelcke. On the operations maps the 9th is usually designated 'Battle Group Colonel Raithel', and shown as being part of III Corps in the 6th Army. The raising of the 9th had come about because the

general commanding the 6th Army, fighting in eastern Austria, had asked for a divisional-sized unit to fill a gap in his battle line. The hastily assembled Battle Group Raithel was the result, and it was put into action on the Semmering Pass in eastern Austria. The 9th passed into American and Russian captivity at the end of the war.

HIGH ALPINE BATTALIONS (HOCHGEBIRGS BATAILLONE)

Wartime experience should have demonstrated to the OKH that there was no need for whole divisions of specially trained Gebirgs soldiers, but Gebirgsjäger formations continued to be raised until the last months of the war. In 1942, experiments demonstrated that standard infantry could operate successfully in mountainous terrain, always provided they were 'stiffened' by Gebirgs units. The OKH then raised specialist high alpine battalions to act as 'stiffeners' for standard infantry conducting operations at high altitudes. Four battalions were raised between July 1942 and November 1943, but the military situation showed that there was no need for such units, whereupon they were stood down and absorbed into standard Gebirgs formations.

GEBIRGS CORPS OF THE ARMY

XV GEBIRGS CORPS

Raised on 12 August 1943 in the Balkans, and served in that theatre of operations throughout the war.

XVIII GEBIRGS CORPS

Formed in Salzburg on 1 April 1938 as XVIII Corps. During December 1941, the description 'Gebirgs' was added to the Corps number. First employed in the Balkans, it was then posted to Lappland. In January 1945, it moved to West Prussia, where it finished the war.

In mountain infantry units, mules replaced vehicles. This mule, with his stretcher-bearer muleteer, is loaded with medical supplies. One box carries ampoules, and the other cotton wool and tablets.

XIX GEBIRGS CORPS

Created in Norway on 1 July 1940 from two units: 21st Group and 3rd Gebirgs Division. First titled Gebirgs Corps 'Norway', it was retitled in November 1942. In 1944 the name changed again to 'Army Detachment Narvik'. The corps was located in Lappland and in southern Norway for the whole of its military life.

XXI GEBIRGS CORPS

Formed in the Balkans during August 1943, it saw service against the Jugoslav partisan army in Croatia, Serbia and Albania.

XXII GEBIRGS CORPS

This formation was raised in Salonika on 20 August 1943, and was one of the reserve units of Army Group E. In April 1944 it was posted to Hungary. At the end of the war, the corps was fighting in eastern Austria, where it passed into captivity.

XXXVI GEBIRGS CORPS

First raised on 19 October 1939, from units in Frontier Control Area No. 14 in Breslau, and given the name Corps Command for Special Purposes. In November 1941, the corps received the title 'Gebirgs'. It fought first in Poland and then in the campaign in the west before moving to Norway, where it spent the rest of the war.

XXXXIX GEBIRGS CORPS

This formation was created on 20 June 1940, but was stood down and not reactivated until October 1940. XXXXIX Corps was selected for the proposed operation to capture the Rock of Gibraltar, but when that mission was aborted, was posted first to Jugoslavia and then to the Eastern Front. In 1942, the corps took part in the advance into the Caucasus and was later destroyed in the fighting in the Crimea. A new XXXXIX Corps was quickly raised, and was posted to Romania. It withdrew under Russian pressure into Moravia, where it surrendered to the Red Army at the end of the war.

LI GEBIRGS CORPS

This was raised on 12 September 1943 in Austria, to replace an infantry corps carrying that number which had been destroyed in the fighting around Stalingrad. The corps served in Italy, particularly in the battles for Cassino.

GEBIRGS DIVISIONS OF THE WAFFEN-SS

6TH SS GEBIRGS DIVISION 'NORD'

Known originally as battle group 'Nord', this unit was raised to the status of a division in June 1942. It served in Lappland from February 1942 until its return to Germany for the Battle of the Bulge in December 1944. Retreating through Germany in the spring of 1945, 'Nord' passed into American captivity.

Composition
11th and 12th SS Gebirgs Regiments

7TH SS FREIWILLIGEN GEBIRGS DIVISION 'PRINZ EUGEN'

The 7th, which was raised on 1 March 1942, was composed mainly of ethnic Germans (Volksdeutsche). Its first operation was against the Jugoslav partisans, and in

Jäger of the 7th SS Gebirgs Division on an anti-partisan sweep in the mountains of Bosnia, 1943.

September 1943 it helped to disarm the Italian forces when Italy left the war. During January 1945, 'Prinz Eugen' began a fighting withdrawal from Jugoslavia and at Cilli the last remnant of the division was captured by partisan forces.

Composition
13th and 14th SS Gebirgs Regiments

13TH WAFFEN GEBIRGS DIVISION OF THE SS 'HANDSCHAR' (CROATIAN NO. 1)

During February 1943, Himmler ordered the creation of a Croat division raised out of Muslim volunteers. The 13th was then put into action on anti-partisan sweeps, chiefly in northern Bosnia. Severe casualties caused the division to be reduced in size to that of a battle group. This served in southern Hungary before retreating into eastern Austria, where it passed into British captivity.

Otto Kumm, Commander of the 7th SS Gebirgs Division 'Prinz Eugen'.

Muslim soldiers of an SS Bosnian Gebirgs Division, operating in Jugoslavia, 1943.

Composition
27th and 28th Gebirgs Regiments

21ST WAFFEN GEBIRGS DIVISION OF THE SS 'SKANDERBEG' (ALBANIAN NO. 1)

Raised by order of Heinrich Himmler on 17 April 1944, the unreliability of the Albanian rank and file in this division was demonstrated during the first anti-partisan sweep, when large numbers of them deserted to the guerrilla forces. This caused the 21st to be reorganized and reduced in numbers. As a reinforcement, nearly 4,000 sailors from the German Navy were drafted into the division. During the German retreat out of Albania, the division was disbanded, with the German Navy contingent being posted to the 7th SS Gebirgs Division, 'Prinz Eugen'.

Composition
50th and 51st SS Gebirgs Regiments

24TH WAFFEN GEBIRGS (KARSTJÄGER) DIVISION OF THE SS

The 24th evolved from a single company which had been created on 10 July 1942 for service in the bare and inhospitable mountain area of the Istrian Peninsula known as the Karst. As early as July 1944, the order came for the unit, now of battalion size, to be expanded to divisional status, but because of a shortage of men that intention could not be realized, and the formation did not expand past the level of a brigade. The 'Karst' Brigade saw action in northern Italy on anti-partisan operations.

Composition
59th SS Gebirgs Karstjäger Regiment

SS GEBIRGS CORPS

V SS GEBIRGS CORPS

Created in Prague during July 1943, with the senior command posts being occupied by officers of the 7th SS Gebirgs Division, 'Prinz Eugen', the corps went into action in the Mostar area during October 1943, and served continuously in the Balkans until the last months of the war, when it was posted to the Eastern Front to serve with the 9th Army.

IX WAFFEN GEBIRGS CORPS OF THE SS (CROATIAN)

The Croatian Gebirgs Corps – composed of the 13th (Handschar) and the 23rd (Kama) – was formed during the summer of 1944. It served as part of the 2nd Panzer Army, which was operating in south-eastern Europe, and surrendered in eastern Austria at the end of the war.

20TH GEBIRGS ARMY

This major formation, which eventually comprised three corps and a reserve division, was first named the 'Lappland Army', and had on strength a number of unconnected military groupings and formations. On 22 June 1942, the Lappland Army's title was changed to '20th Gebirgs', and by the end of December 1944, all German troops stationed in Norway were under its command.

The order of battle of the Lappland Army in February 1942 was:

Gebirgs Corps 'Norway'	2nd and 6th Gebirgs Divisions
XXXVI Corps	163rd and 169th Infantry Divisions
III (Finnish) Corps	6th SS Gebirgs Division 'Nord' and 3rd Finnish Division
Army Reserve	7th Gebirgs Division

Inevitably, there were changes in composition as, for example, when III (Finnish) Corps, which had been under German command, reverted back to Finnish command.

In April 1945, the order of battle of 20th Gebirgs Army was:

XXXVI Corps	Panzer Brigade 'Norway', Machine Gun Ski Battalion 'Finland'
LXX Corps	613rd, 274th and 280th Divisions
XXXIII Corps	295th and 702nd Infantry Divisions, and the 14th Luftwaffe Division
LXXI Corps	230th and 210th Infantry Divisions, the Fortress Brigade 'Lofoten' 139th Brigade, 140th Brigade and 503rd Brigade
XIX Corps	(also known as Army Detachment 'Narvik') 193rd Brigade, 270th Division, 6th Gebirgs Division, Cyclist Reconnaissance Battalion
Army Reserve	7th Gebirgs Division

GRENADIER DIVISIONS OF THE WAFFEN-SS

14TH WAFFENGRENADIER DIVISION OF THE SS (GALICIAN NO. 1)

First called the SS Volunteer Division (Galicia) in July 1943, the formation was renamed the 14th Volunteer Grenadier Division (Galicia No. 1) in June 1944. Although not completely raised, the division's regiments were soon in action, and during the battle for Lemberg the 14th was nearly destroyed. Re-raised in the autumn of 1944, the 14th helped put down the mutiny of the Slovak Army, and in February 1945 the division was ordered to hand over all weapons to German paratroops and to prepare to convert to the status of a paratroop division. The military situation made that order redundant, and in Austria the division surrendered to the Americans.

In 1943, the composition of the division was: SS Freiwilligen Regiment No. 1, SS Freiwilligen Regiment No. 2 and SS Freiwilligen Regiment No. 3.

The change in name from 'Freiwilligen' to 'Grenadier' changed the regimental names and numbers, and these were then: Grenadier Regiment No. 29, Grenadier Regiment No. 30 and Grenadier Regiment No. 31.

15TH WAFFENGRENADIER DIVISION OF THE SS (LATVIAN NO. 1)

Hitler ordered the raising of a Latvian SS Legion in February 1943, and the first name, Latvian SS Volunteer Legion, was changed to the 15th Latvian SS Volunteer Division, and finally to the title shown above. Before the division was fully raised, some of its units were in action, and by the end of 1943 the whole division was embattled. It was severely mauled in the fighting around Novo-Sokolniki, and conducted a fighting retreat through Latvia. In the spring of 1944 the division, now re-formed, was put back into action, and it fought in West Prussia, where the remnant of the 15th surrendered to the Red Army.

The composition of the 15th was: Waffengrenadier Regiment No. 32 (Latvian No. 3), Waffengrenadier Regiment No. 33 (Latvian No. 4) and Waffengrenadier Regiment No. 34 (Latvian No. 5).

19TH WAFFENGRENADIER DIVISION OF THE SS (LATVIAN NO. 2)

On 7 January 1944, the 2nd SS Latvian Division was raised as the 19th Latvian SS Volunteer Division, and in May received its second and final title, as shown above.

The division fought in the Leningrad area, and took part in the fighting retreat from that area as well as in five of the six battles in Courland before surrendering in May 1945 to the Russians.

The composition of the division was: SS Waffengrenadier Regiment No. 42 (Latvian No. 1), SS Waffengrenadier Regiment No. 43 (Latvian No. 2) and SS Waffengrenadier Regiment No. 44 (Latvian No. 6).

20TH WAFFENGRENADIER DIVISION OF THE SS (ESTONIAN NO. 1)

On 1 October 1942, an Estonian Legion was created, and was originally conceived as a motorized infantry regiment. The flow of recruits enabled the legion to be expanded to become the 3rd Estonian SS Volunteer Brigade, and then, during January 1944, to the status of 2nd Estonian SS Volunteer Division. It was soon in action on the Eastern Front, and was split into battle groups which served with other divisions. In September 1944 the division regrouped, and went into action during January 1945 around Breslau. Near there, the mass of the 20th was encircled, and surrendered to the Russians.

The composition of the division was: SS Volunteer Grenadier Regiment No. 42, later in 1945, renumbered No. 45 (Estonian No. 1); No. 43, later renumbered in 1945 No. 46 (Estonian No. 2), and No. 47 (not raised until November 1944) and titled 'Estonian No. 3' in 1945.

25TH WAFFENGRENADIER DIVISION OF THE SS 'HUNYADI' (HUNGARIAN NO. 1)

Raised by order of Heinrich Himmler in April 1944 as the 'SS Freiwilligen Grenadier Division in Hungary', it was almost immediately put into action, first against the Red Army, and then, in the spring of 1945, against the US Army, to which the division surrendered at the end of the war.

The composition of the division was: SS Grenadier Regiment No. 61, SS Grenadier Regiment No. 62 and SS Grenadier Regiment No. 63.

26TH WAFFENGRENADIER DIVISION OF THE SS

The first intent, to raise a Panzer division out of the 49th SS Panzer Grenadier Brigade, was not proceeded with, and in March 1945 a fresh and successful attempt was made to create a division out of Hungarian Army units.

The composition of the division was: SS Waffengrenadier Regiment No. 64, SS Waffengrenadier Regiment No. 65 and SS Waffengrenadier Regiment No. 85.

27TH SS FREIWILLIGEN GRENADIER DIVISION 'LANGEMARCK'

The 27th Legion was upgraded to brigade status in May 1943, and was in action late in December of that year in the Ukraine. Encircled near Zhitomir, the brigade lost 50 per cent of its effectives, and was re-raised in April 1944. In September, the brigade was again expanded to divisional status, and was in action in the Battle of the Bulge in December 1944. The division was posted to the Eastern Front, where it surrendered to the Red Army in May 1945.

The composition of the division was: SS Freiwilligen Grenadier Regiment No. 66, SS Freiwilligen Grenadier Regiment No. 67 and SS Freiwilligen Grenadier Regiment No. 68.

29TH WAFFENGRENADIER DIVISION OF THE SS (ITALIAN NO. 1)

Created out of militia battalions, later regiments which had been raised by Mussolini's Socialist regime in northern Italy, this formation was then expanded into a Waffengrenadier Brigade, and in April 1945, upgraded to divisional status.

The composition of the division was: SS Infantry Regiment No. 1, SS Infantry Regiment No. 2 and an officers' battalion.

30TH WAFFENGRENADIER DIVISION OF THE SS (RUSSIAN NO. 2)

This formation grew out of the Russian Home Defence units raised by the SS during the summer of 1944.

The division's 1st regiment consisted of the former Home Defence battalions 57, 60, 61 and the Minsk Police area command; the 2nd Regiment was made up of the former 62nd, 63rd and 64th Battalions and the Lida Police area command; the 3rd Regiment came from the Slusk Police area; and the 4th Regiment came from the Police area of the Pripet marshes. In August, the brigade, which was composed of Slav personnel, was transferred from the Police authority to that of the SS. The formation served on the Western Front, and suffered heavy losses. In January 1945, the weakened formation was disbanded, and some of its units were posted to other SS units.

The composition of the division, which had been known as the 1st, 2nd and 3rd Regiments of the Home Defence Battalions in September 1944, became in October of that year: SS Waffengrenadier Regiment No. 75, SS Waffengrenadier Regiment No. 76 and SS Waffengrenadier Regiment No. 77.

31ST SS FREIWILLIGEN GRENADIER DIVISION

The intention to raise a division from Volksdeutsche living in the Batschka met with many difficulties. The detachments which were raised were formed into battle groups and fought with similar groups of the Army against the Red Army, which was advancing through Hungary. After suffering heavy losses in the battle for Pecs, the remnants of the division marched to Marburg in Jugoslavia, where it was fleshed out with groups of soldiers from disbanded units. The division was rushed to Silesia in February 1945, and after a fighting retreat, was surrounded in Königgrätz in Czechoslovakia, and surrendered.

The composition of the division was: SS Freiwilligen Grenadier Regiment No. 79 and SS Freiwilligen Grenadier Regiment No. 80.

32ND SS FREIWILLIGEN GRENADIER DIVISION '30 JANUARY'

In January 1945, the first companies of the future division were assembled and given the title 'Battlegroup Kurmark', later SS Regiment No. 32. The soldiers were drawn from a number of miscellaneous units. The first operational area was on the eastern bank of the River Oder, fighting against Red Army units in the bridgeheads around Frankfurt.

An SS trooper waving his men forward during the Battle of the Bulge, 1944. On his belt he is wearing his entrenching tool, and on his back the Sturmgepäck. In the background are burning American vehicles.

As the units of the incompletely raised division arrived, they were put into action so that the 32nd fought for only a brief time as a complete formation. Put into an operation to relieve Berlin, the regiments were surrounded, and only a few isolated splinter groups escaped and fought their way through to the 12th Army's position. The fragments of the 32nd surrendered to the Americans on the River Elbe

The composition of the division was: SS Freiwilligen Grenadier Regiment No. 86, SS Freiwilligen Grenadier Regiment No. 87 and SS Freiwilligen Grenadier Regiment No. 88.

33RD WAFFENGRENADIER DIVISION OF THE SS 'CHARLEMAGNE' (FRENCH NO. 1)

Raised during August 1943 as the French SS Volunteer Grenadier Regiment, this SS unit had an Army predecessor, the 'Légion Volontaire Française'. The first military operation of this SS division was against the Red Army forces which had broken through at Sanok. That and succeeding battles caused heavy casualties. In November 1944, the Waffengrenadier Regiment, by now a brigade, was regrouped and retrained, and preparations began to raise it to divisional status. Before concentration could be completed, the swift advance of the Red Army caused the 33rd to be committed to action piecemeal, and usually under the command of a German Army unit. In the area around Köslin, the division was regrouped and almost immediately encircled. Nearly 2,000 men escaped the encirclement and reached the Baltic Sea, where they fought in operations around Swinemünde and Danzig. These remnants then carried out a fighting withdrawal to Schleswig-Holstein, where they surrendered to the British Army. Other splinter groups of the 33rd fought along the Danube, and passed into American captivity.

The organization of the division in the autumn of 1944 was: Grenadier Regiment No. 1 and Grenadier Regiment No. 2; and in February 1945 it was Waffengrenadier Regiment No. 57 and Waffengrenadier Regiment No. 58.

34TH SS GRENADIER DIVISION 'LANDSTORM NEDERLAND'

This formation was raised as a territorial national defence organization officered by German policemen. In November 1944, the title changed to SS Freiwilligen Grenadier Brigade 'Landstorm Nederland', and during March 1945 the brigade was raised to the status of a division.

The organization of the brigade in the autumn of 1944 was SS Freiwilligen Grenadier Regiment No. 83 (Dutch No. 3) and SS Freiwilligen Grenadier Regiment No. 84 (Dutch No. 4), and in March 1945 a third regiment was added which raised the formation to the status of a division: SS Grenadier Regiment 'Klotz'.

35TH SS POLICE GRENADIER DIVISION

Raised from units of the police training college at Dresden to form a brigade, this was raised to divisional status, with the officers for the new formation coming from the SS Junkerschule in Braunschweig. The brigade was composed of the 1st and 2nd Police Regiments, which were changed during March 1945 to become SS Police Regiments Nos 89 and 90. A third regiment, created in 1942 in Russia, was retitled and became SS Police Regiment No. 91. The division, which was put into action to fight down the Red Army formations which had broken through in the area between Cottbus and Berlin, was smashed, and the survivors surrendered to the Red Army at the end of the war.

The organization of the division was: SS Police Grenadier Regiment No. 1 (later the

89th), SS Police Grenadier Regiment No. 2 (later the 90th) and SS Police Grenadier Regiment No. 3 (later the 91st).

36TH WAFFENGRENADIER DIVISION OF THE SS

This notorious unit was first created around a nucleus of criminals in June 1940. From that date until the autumn of 1944, 'Dr Dirlewanger's Special Group' was put into action and carried out atrocities in Poland and on the Eastern Front. Their military duties were anti-partisan sweeps. The 'Special Group', subsequently known as the 'Dirlewanger Brigade', took part in the fighting in Warsaw, and the heavy losses which it suffered were made good by taking on strength other military criminals. After putting down the mutiny in Slovakia, the brigade was posted to the River Oder front, and during February 1945 it was raised to divisional status. The 36th was surrounded in the Halbe pocket, and was taken prisoner by the Red Army.

The composition of the brigade in 1944 was: Regiment No. 1 and Regiment No. 2.

CHAPTER FIVE

MISCELLANEOUS INFANTRY FORMATIONS

There were several minor groupings which were considered to be on the infantry establishment. These were not actually organized by regiments or divisions, but by battalions, and included the following.

FORTRESS (FESTUNGS) UNITS

The title of 'Fortress' was a misnomer, as these were infantry units. The 35 battalions of Festungstruppen were raised in two waves: 22 in one wave, and 13 in another.

The Fortress formations were used mainly for local guard duties, and their battalion title included the identifying description 'County Rifles' (Landesschützen).

RESERVE DIVISIONS

These were not divisions in the accepted sense of that term, but a divisional staff whose task it was to find draftees for units in the field.

The Reserve Divisions were numbered: 141, 143, 148, 151, 153, 154, 155 (Panzer), 156, 157, 158, 159, 165, 166, 169, 171, 173, 174, 179 (Panzer), 182, 187, 188 (Gebirgs), 189, 191 and 233 (Panzer).

TRAINING DIVISIONS (FELDAUSBILDUNGSDIVISIONEN)

Numbered: 381, 382, 388, 390 and 391.

FRONTIER GUARD (GRENZWACHT) FORMATIONS

These were numbered: 537, 538, 539 and 540.

GERMAN AIR FORCE DIVISIONS (LUFTWAFFE FELDDIVISIONEN)

In the autumn of 1942, a number of Luftwaffe ground staffs, Flak units and recruit depots were transferred *en bloc* to become Army infantry. Their numbers were sufficient to form 22 divisions of Jäger-style infantry.

The order of battle of a German Air Force division was two Jäger regiments, each of three battalions. Divisional strength was about 10,000 all ranks.

PARTY MILITIAS

In the last year of the war and in the aftermath of the failed bomb plot of July 1944, Hitler distrusted his senior commanders of the Army, and gave military responsibility to leaders of the Nazi Party while at the same time denying such responsibility to the military. General Fromm, who was executed for his part in the assassination attempt, was replaced as Commander of the Ersatz Army, and that

Fighting is thirsty work, and one of the two paratroopers in this photograph takes a draught from his water bottle. The other man, keeping watch, has a grenade-projector cup fitted to the muzzle of his rifle.

post was given to Heinrich Himmler, Head of the SS. Thus, from autumn 1944, the SS controlled the flow of replacements to units in the field.

As the war situation deteriorated, Hitler turned more and more to the Nazi Party, and organized a Volkssturm ('People's Army'). This was the first of many attempts at creating military formations which were outside Army control, because those new formations were raised, organized and fielded by the party itself. As a self-confessed revolutionary, Hitler was convinced that political fanaticism, the expression of the will, could produce victory; determined to create that spirit, he introduced the word 'Volks' ('People's') into unit titles. It was his belief that this word would imbue the men of any unit so named with National Socialist fervour.

In addition to the party-raised Volkssturm, there were Army infantry, Gebirgsjäger and other standard military units which had the term 'Volks' attached to them. That move was followed by the raising of Volksgrenadier divisions, to which a higher than normal issue of fast-firing machine guns and machine pistols was given in order to compensate for their lower establishments of men.

In the last few months of the war, special 'Adolf Hitler' militias were raised, and some of these were put into action. It was during this period that the German partisan movement (Wehrwolf) was created. Its units were well trained, but the force lacked direction from the centre, and the units in the field had no influence on the course of Allied military operations.

With the exception of the Army divisions whose description included the word 'Volks' (the Volksgebirgsjäger) and which were therefore part of the field Army, these other units – the Volkssturm, the Adolf Hitler militias and the Wehrwolf – were Nazi Party bodies, and not being part of the Army, will not be described in this text.

A paratroop machine gun post in Tunisia, late 1942. The weapon is the MG 34 in its light machine gun mode.

AIRBORNE (FALLSCHIRMJÄGER) FORMATIONS

1ST PARA (FALLSCHIRMJÄGER) DIVISION

This was created during April 1943 out of the 7th Flieger Division, the original airborne formation. The 1st fought in Sicily and in Italy, being heavily involved in the defence of Cassino.

Composition
Fallschirmjäger Regiments 1, 3 and 4

2ND PARA (FALLSCHIRMJÄGER) DIVISION

Raised during 1943, this was first put into action in Italy, where, among other missions, it took part in the rescue of Mussolini. Late in 1943, it carried out a parachute drop on the island of Leros, and captured it. The 2nd was then posted to the Eastern Front, but returned to the Western Front, where it was destroyed in the battle for Brest in 1944. Re-raised in October 1944, the new 2nd Para then fought in Holland, and finished the war in western Germany.

A recruiting poster for the German airborne forces.

Composition
Fallschirmjäger Regiments 2, 6 and 7

3RD PARA (FALLSCHIRMJÄGER) DIVISION

Raised in France during the last months of 1943, its order of battle should have included the 5th Regiment, but that formation was posted to Tunisia, where it was destroyed. A reconstituted 5th Regiment was raised and taken onto establishment during March 1944.

Composition
The new Fallschirmjäger Regiment 5, and Regiments 8 and 9.

4TH PARA (FALLSCHIRMJÄGER) DIVISION

Raised in Italy during the last months of 1943, this division fought in that theatre of operations.

Composition
Fallschirmjäger Regiments 10, 11 and 12. Also on the divisional order of battle were elements from two Italian Para Divisions: Folgore and Demgo.

5TH PARA (FALLSCHIRMJÄGER) DIVISION

Raised in April 1944, the 5th fought on the Western Front, where it was soon destroyed. It then fragmented into battle groups, the last of which fought in the Ruhr.

Composition
Fallschirmjäger Regiments 13, 14 and 15

Paratroops of Koch's regiment marching through the streets of Tunis shortly after they had been airlifted to Tunisia in November 1942.

German paratroop recruits had to carry out a number of drops before they were considered trained soldiers and issued with the jump badge. In this photograph, Adi Strauch's group of recruits are preparing to make their qualifying jump (Strauch is marked with a cross).

A pre-war training exercise: paratroops who have just landed concentrate around an MG 34 which has been set up in the heavy machine gun mode on a tripod.

6TH PARA (FALLSCHIRMJÄGER) DIVISION

Raised during April 1944, it was put into action on the Western Front, where it was destroyed. A new 6th Division was raised during the last months of 1944 with the same order of battle. The 16th Regiment fought in Normandy and then on the Eastern Front, before returning to fight with the division in France and in Holland. The 6th Division surrendered to the British Army at the end of the war.

Composition

Fallschirmjäger Regiments 16, 17 and 18

7TH PARA (FALLSCHIRMJÄGER) DIVISION

This formation was created out of fragments of para formations which had been destroyed in battle. During October 1944, it was given the task of building a defensive front along the Albert Canal in Belgium, which it held until it was withdrawn into western Germany, where it was destroyed.

Composition

Fallschirmjäger Regiments 19, 20 and 21

8TH PARA (FALLSCHIRMJÄGER) DIVISION

The order for this formation to be raised was issued during September 1944, but was revoked and not reissued until January 1945. The 23rd Regiment did not serve with 8th Para Division, its parent formation, but with 2nd Para Division. Because of the military situation, a 24th regiment was never raised. As a replacement for the 23rd Regiment the division received 1st Assault Battalion. The 8th took part in the defence of the Rhine,

A team of mortar men from an airborne unit, in action in Normandy, 1944.

and after a fighting retreat into northern Germany, surrendered to the British at the end of the war.

Composition
Fallschirmjäger Regiments 22, 23 and 24

9TH PARA (FALLSCHIRMJÄGER) DIVISION

The proposal made in September 1944 to raise a 9th Fallschirmjäger Division was not acted upon until January 1945. Because of the deteriorating military situation, to begin with only battalions could be raised. Some divisional units fought in the defence of Breslau, and others were transferred to the 23rd SS Division. The remnant of the division fought a retreat back through Germany, was involved in the battle for Berlin, and surrendered to the British in northern Germany.

Composition
Fallschirmjäger Regiments 25, 26 and 27

10TH PARA (FALLSCHIRMJÄGER) DIVISION

The order issued in September 1944 to raise the 10th Para Division was revoked and not reissued until February 1945. The division was posted to eastern Austria, where it was destroyed around Feldbach. Remnants of the 10th escaped and carried on the fight in Czechoslovakia, where they surrendered to the Russians.

Composition
Fallschirmjäger Regiments 28, 29 and 30

Men of a German airborne unit resting at the conclusion of an assault on the Corinth Canal, 1941.
The dark-coloured band worn round the helmet served not only as an identification, but when filled with foliage was a form of camouflage.

Baron von der Heydte, commander of the 6th Fallschirmjäger Regiment, liaising in Normandy with SS officers of the 17th Division.

11TH PARA (FALLSCHIRMJÄGER) DIVISION

The order to create an 11th Para Division was issued in March 1945, but the formation was never raised, and those units which were formed fought as battle groups in Holland, where they surrendered to the British at the end of the war.

Composition
Fallschirmjäger Regiments 37, 38 and 39

PARA (FALLSCHIRMJÄGER) CORPS

The original Airborne Corps, raised immediately before the outbreak of the Second World War, was numbered XI, and was composed of the Luftwaffe's 7th Flieger Division and the Army's 22nd (Air-landing) Division.

Eleventh Corps fought in the campaign in the west in 1940, and in the invasion of Crete. Because the 22nd (Air-landing) Division was unavailable for that operation, the 5th Gebirgs Division was brought in as a substitute. When, in January 1944, the idea of a Para Army was proposed and then accepted, the XI Corps was renumbered to become I Corps, with the 1st and 2nd Fallschirmjäger Divisions under command (the divisional structure is set out on pages 62–3). The life of I Para Corps was spent in Italy.

The II Para Corps was created on 12 May 1944, and had the 3rd and 5th Fallschirmjäger

Divisions under command. It fought on the Western Front.

PARA (FALLSCHIRMJÄGER) ARMY

The order to form the 1st Para Army was issued by the Luftwaffe High Command during March 1944, and the raising of that major formation was completed by the end of August.

The Para Army was employed on the Western Front, and served without break from September 1944 until the end of the war in May 1945.

SECURITY DIVISIONS (SICHERUNGSDIVISIONEN)

To ensure the security of rear areas of the armies fighting on the Eastern Front, special infantry divisions were organized. Most of these were made up of poor-quality soldiers, often men from the older age groups, many of whom had fought in the First World War. The arms issued were initially either of obsolete pattern or else were captured materiel. The order of battle of a Sicherungsdivision was for just two infantry regiments, one employed on active or sweep operations, and a second one, of even lower-grade personnel, to carry out guard duties in the division's static areas.

Each division had support formations, including a light artillery battalion, pioneers and supply detachments. Some security formations were reinforced by a motorized police battalion. Security divisions were employed on the Eastern Front, and each Army Group was allocated one or more of them. Army Group South also had units of Hungarian security troops under its command.

It must be admitted that the security divisions had a hopeless task to fulfil. Their establishments were low, they were poorly armed, and they had vast areas of countryside to control. One division had to guard more than 31,000 square miles of heavily wooded marshland which was heavily infested with partisan groups. That vast area was larger in extent than the whole of Austria.

The operations plans for the attack upon the Soviet Union appreciated that there would be a need for an increase in the number of Sicherungs divisions. This could be achieved either by expanding brigades to divisional size, or else by converting standard infantry divisions into Sicherungs formations. Although the intention was that the divisions would have only security duties to perform, several of them were caught up in major military operations and were put into action as standard infantry divisions.

The Sicherungs divisions were numbered: 201, 203, 207, 213, 221, 281, 284, 285, 286, 403, 442, 444, 454 and 455.

CHAPTER SIX

INFANTRY WEAPONS

The standard weapon of the German Army, particularly the infantry arm, was the Gewehr 98, which had been in service since the end of the nineteenth century. This five-round, bolt-operated gun had been the principal firearm of the German Army during the First World War, and remained so for most of the Second. In the middle years of the war, this weapon was to be phased out in favour of a semi-automatic rifle, but with the increasingly wide distribution of machine pistols, that phasing out became unnecessary.

THE GEWEHR 98 AND KARABINER 98

Calibre	7.92 mm
Length	126 cm (Gewehr and Karabiner); 110 cm (Karabiner 98 K)
Weight	4 kg approx.
Magazine	Five rounds loaded in a single clip
Operation	Bolt-action, manually operated
Range	800 m
Sidearm	A bayonet or a grenade-projector could be fitted

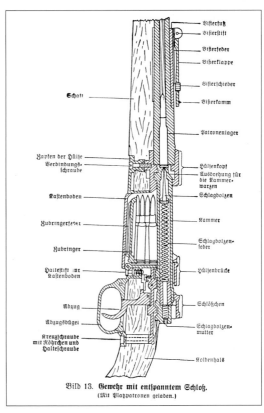

Bild 13. Gewehr mit entspanntem Schloß.
(Mit Platzpatronen geladen.)

A cut-away drawing of a rifle with its chamber loaded with a drill cartridge.

THE GEWEHR 3/40

This was a short rifle designed for paratroops, and had a folding stock. In every other respect it was similar in design to the 98 models.

THE GEWEHR 41

This was a semi-automatic rifle made in two models, the Gewehr 41 M and the Gewehr 41 W. The main difference between the two types was in their construction.

An SS recruit undergoing instruction in musketry.

Calibre	7.92 mm
Length	114 cm
Weight	4.9 kg
Magazine	Two five-round clips fitted into a magazine on the side of the rifle
Operation	Semi-automatic
Range	1,300 m

THE FALLSCHIRMJÄGERGEWEHR 42

The Model 42 was not so much an automatic rifle as a light machine gun. It had a permanently fitted folding bipod, and fired either single shots or automatic. A safety catch was fitted.

Calibre	7.92 mm
Length	111 cm when fitted with a bayonet
Weight	4 kg
Magazine	A twenty-round magazine was fitted on the left side of the body
Range	1,300 m

THE KARABINER 43

This semi-automatic rifle was a development of the Gewehr 41, but was lighter in weight by nearly 0.5 kg.

MACHINE PISTOLS

THE MP 38 AND 40 (SCHMEISSER)

There was no difference in the operation of the two weapons, only in the external appearance. The 38 had a smooth case, and the 40 a ridged one. The earlier pattern suffered from the defect that there was no safety catch, but merely a notch into which the cocking handle fitted. The MP 40 remained the standard-issue weapon until the end of the war.

Calibre	9 mm
Length	85 cm
Weight	4 kg without the magazine

70

The Volksgewehr was introduced so late in the war that very few were issued before the end of hostilities.

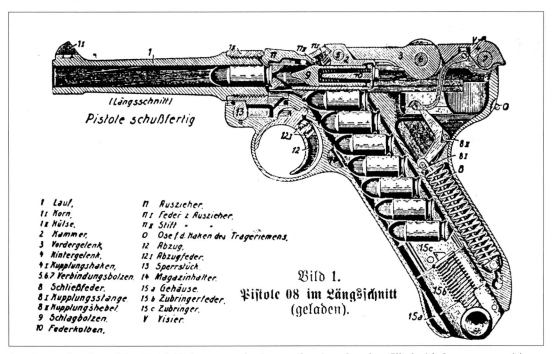

(Längsschnitt)

Pistole schußfertig

1 Lauf.	11 Auszieher.
11 Korn.	111 Feder z Auszieher.
111 Hülse.	111 Stift . .
2 Kammer.	0 Ose f.d. Haken des Trageriemens.
3 Vordergelenk.	12 Abzug.
4 Hintergelenk.	121 Abzugfeder.
41 Kupplungshaken.	13 Sperrstück.
5.6.7 Verbindungsbolzen.	14 Magazinhalter.
8 Schließfeder.	15 a Gehäuse.
81 Kupplungsstange.	15 b Zubringerfeder.
811 Kupplungshebel.	15 c Zubringer.
9 Schlagbolzen.	V Visier.
10 Federkolben.	

Bild 1.
Pistole 08 im Längsschnitt
(geladen).

A cut-away drawing of the Pistol 08, known as the Luger, showing chamber filled with 9 mm ammunition.

Magazine	32 rounds
Rate of fire	500 r.p.m. cyclic; 150 r.p.m. practical
Range	100 m using the battle sight; 210 m using the folding rear sight

THE MP 43 MACHINE PISTOL

This was a revolutionary weapon because its components were made of stamped metal, not machined parts. It also fired standard rifle/machine gun rounds of 7.92 mm calibre,

The MP 38 was one of the first machine pistols introduced into the services. Its replacement, the MP 40 shown here, was an improved version of the MP 38.

A light machine gun post in the snow of the Eastern Front, 1944.

The Sturmgewehr was introduced into service during 1943, but its production was halted, and it was not reintroduced until 1944.

The standard machine gun, with which the German forces entered the Second World War, was the MG 34, seen here in its light machine gun mode on a bipod.

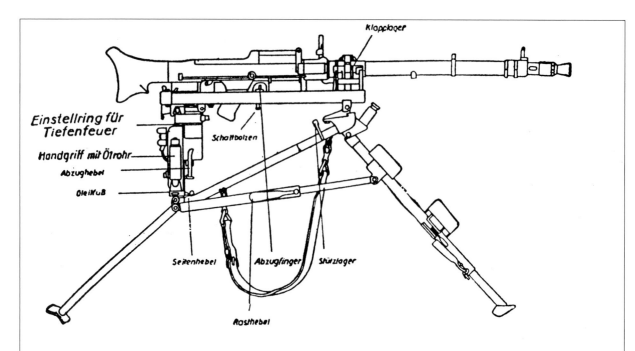

Two drawings of the standard machine gun, the MG 34, in heavy machine gun mode, mounted on a tripod.

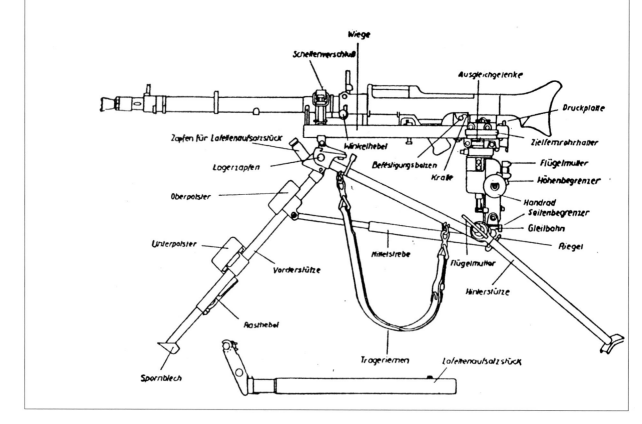

but filled with a lower charge to reduce recoil. The MP 43 suffered from the defect that it was heavy to carry and was unreliable in action.

Calibre	7.92 mm (a short version of rifle ammunition was fired)
Length	94 cm
Weight	5 kg
Magazine	38 rounds loaded into a slightly curved magazine
Sights	Leaf rear sight
Range	870 m

THE STURMGEWEHR 44

This weapon was intended to be the main short-range machine pistol of the German Army, but too few were issued to be an effective replacement. Regulations for firing the Sturmgewehr laid down that a burst of fire should not exceed five rounds because of the high recoil vibration.

Calibre	7.92 mm (a short version of rifle ammunition was fired)
Length	94 cm
Weight	5.6 kg

MACHINE GUNS

The MG 34 was the standard machine gun on issue to the German forces, and remained so until it was phased out through the introduction of the MG 42. That piece was itself superseded by the MG 45, also known as the M 3. All three weapons could be fired as a light machine-gun (LMG) or heavy machine gun (HMG). The change from LMG to HMG mode was brought about by being mounted on a tripod.

Calibre	7.92 mm (7.62 mm in the case of the MG 45)
Length	122 cm
Weight	12 kg when bipod-mounted as a light machine gun
	19 kg when mounted on a tripod in heavy machine gun mode
Feed	Linked metal belt or drum
Rate of fire	900 r.p.m. (cyclic) as a light machine gun
	300 r.p.m. (cyclic) as a heavy machine gun (the later versions, the MG 42 and 45, both had higher rates of fire)
Range	600–800 m (LMG)
	2,000–2,500 m (HMG)

GRENADE LAUNCHER (SCHIESSBECHER)

This cup-shaped launcher could be fitted to any rifle in service. It fired small grenades – high-explosive smoke or flare as well as anti-tank.

It consisted of a short 30 mm barrel which screwed onto the muzzle of the rifle and was retained in place by a pair of fastening hooks. There was a grenade sight on the left hand side of the rifle, and it was calibrated to fire over ranges from 50 to 250 m.

The grenade in the launcher was projected by means of a special blank cartridge. One man in a section of ten carried the Schiessbecher grenade launcher, and he also carried 10 high-explosive and 5 anti-tank grenades.

ROCKET-PROPELLED WEAPONS

In the middle years of the war there was a dramatic change in German tactics when fighting against Allied armour. This was brought about by the introduction into service of rocket-propelled grenades which could be fired either by one man or a team of two. These weapons were short-range, which meant that the enemy armoured fighting vehicles had to be attacked at close quarters.

THE PANZERFAUST 30 OR FAUSTPATRONE 2

This was the first of the weapons series which launched rocket-propelled grenades. Effective

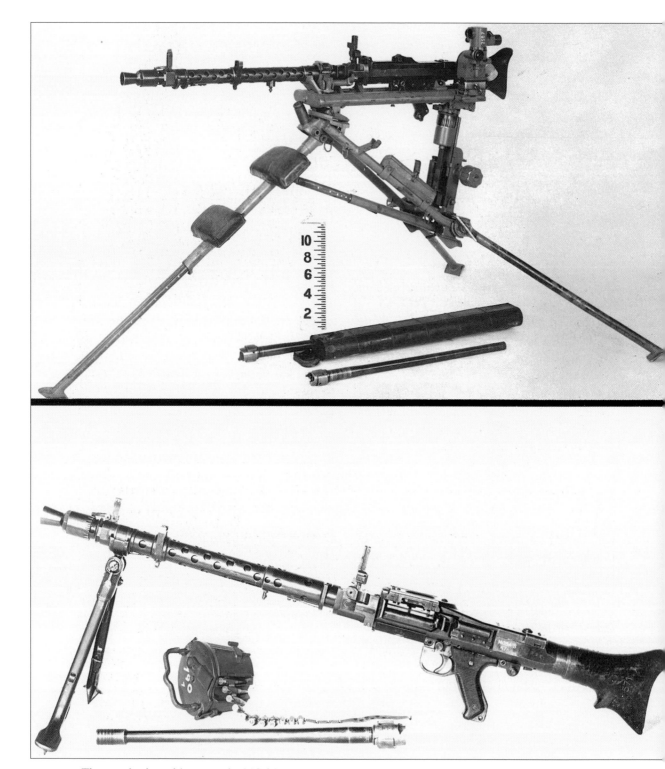

The standard machine gun, the MG 34. It is shown here mounted on a tripod in its heavy machine gun mode and on a bipod in light machine gun mode.

The successor to the MG 34 was the MG 42, which had an increased rate of fire. It is shown here in the light machine gun mode on a bipod.

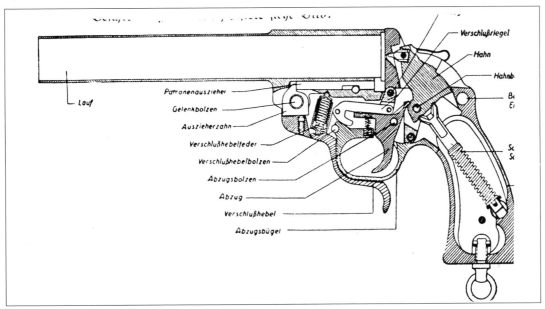

A cut-away drawing of the German Army flare pistol. Later versions of this weapon were rebored to fire small grenades.

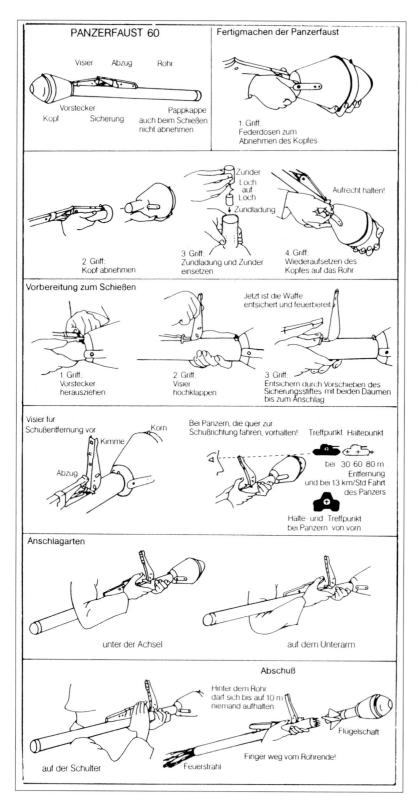

A page from a German training manual showing how the Panzerfaust 60 was to be armed and fired.

Paratroopers bringing forward fresh supplies of the single-shot Panzerfaust.

range was about 30 m, and at that distance the grenade could penetrate 18 cm of armour.

The Panzerfaust 30 consisted of a hollow steel firing tube, 2 cm in diameter. A turnip-headed bomb was placed inside the firing tube, and the head of the bomb projected from the top end of it. The base of the bomb consisted of a shaft filled with a propellant charge and fitted with stabilizing fins.

The total weight of the Panzerfaust 30 was only 5 kg, so this light and mobile weapon could be fired from a variety of positions: prone, kneeling, standing with the weapon resting on the firer's shoulder or across his right arm. The sighting mechanism was crude: a vertical piece of metal fitted near the end of the firing tube.

Before a grenade was placed into the firing tube, its steel fins were wrapped around the propellant shaft. Upon being fired, those spring-activated fins opened and held the grenade on its flight path. The action of firing produced a stream of flame which propelled the bomb. Like all Panzerfaust weapons, this was a single-shot piece. Once used, the hollow firing tube was discarded.

In the operations carried out during the winter of 1944/5, the German Army in the east was fighting on its own soil. Battle groups of men were put into action armed with Panzerfaust rocket weapons, and ordered to hold back the tank masses of the Red Army which were sweeping across the German countryside.

THE PANZERFAUST 40 KLEIN

This was a smaller version of the Faustpatrone, and had a lower penetrating power.

THE PANZERFAUST 60

This had an apertured sight for 30, 60 and 90 m, a redesigned firing mechanism and a thicker firing tube to compensate for the stronger propellant charge. The weapon's weight was thereby increased to 6.4 kg. The bomb of the Panzerfaust 60 could penetrate 25 cm of armour.

THE PANZERFAUST 100

This was the final design, and was a slightly larger version of the 60 model. This type had a range of 150 m.

THE RAKETEN PANZERBÜCHSE 5

The Panzerfaust models were all fired by a single soldier, but there was also a two-man anti-tank rocket weapon, the Raketen Panzerbüchse 5, also known as the 'tank terror' (Panzerschreck). Because of its shape, it was also called the Stovepipe (Ofenrohr). This weapon projected an 88 mm missile from a firing tube by means of an electrical firing mechanism. The weapon consisted of a hollow tube fitted with a fore and back sight, a cocking lever and a trigger. The missile it discharged was a 3 kg grenade with a propellant in its tail. The grenade was placed in the rear of the tube, and was held in position by a catch which made contact with the electrical leads at the rear of the launcher.

To fire the weapon, the trigger was pressed, an action which, by activating a magnetized rod, produced a spark which ignited the propellant charge. A fixed tail fin, circular in shape, kept the bomb on its correct flight path.

The first models of the Panzerschreck were made with no steel protective shields, but these were added to later versions. The shield, which was fitted to protect the firer from the stream of propellant flame, had a small

Towards the end. Grenadiers are carried up the line in open trucks. They are armed with the single-shot Panzerfaust anti-tank projectiles.

A German paratrooper ready to fire the Panzerschreck anti-tank rocket launcher. This is the later version of the weapon, for it has an observation panel in the protective shield.

window on its left side through which the firer aimed the weapon. In action, one man loaded the bomb into the rear end of the firing tube and then patted the firer on the shoulder to let him know that the weapon was loaded; he then moved to one side, firstly to remove himself from the path of the stream of flame that was projected, and secondly to observe whether a hit had been scored. If it had not, he then loaded a second grenade into the firing tube. Unlike the Panzerfaust series, the Panzerschreck could be re-used.

When the rocket was fitted inside the tube, its 64 cm length took up nearly half the length of the 164 cm tube. The effective range of the Panzerschreck was about 130 m.

THE RAKETENWERFER 43 OR PÜPPCHEN

This was a wheeled version of the Panzerschreck. It was of the same calibre, but the wheeled carriage raised its weight to 122 kg. The carriage had a single trail, and was fitted with a protective shield. The breech block of the Püppchen was of a simple hinged type fitted with a striker mechanism, but there was no facility to traverse or to elevate. Traversing was effected along a slide, and elevation was achieved by a spade handgrip. The sighting system was a fixed foresight and an adjustable rear sight, which was mounted on the barrel. The sight was graduated for ranges between 190 and 760 m. The grenade fired was the standard anti-tank projectile, but was unusual because when it was fitted, its base cap, which served also as a cartridge cap, remained in the breech and had to be removed before the next round could be loaded.

Development of the Püppchen was so slow that only a few weapons of this type were completed, and these did not come into service until late in 1944. There was a

The improvement on the Panzerschreck was a wheeled version known as the 'Püppchen'. It is seen in this photograph being operated by a British soldier.

later version of the Püppchen: the 'Tank Death' (Panzertod). This weapon was intended to project a 105 mm 3 kg bomb over a distance of 500 m. The end of the war in May 1945, coupled with the late invention of the weapon, meant that it never entered service.

GRENADES AND MORTARS

HAND GRENADES

In the German Army the hand grenade was called the 'poor man's mortar' because it was a high-trajectory weapon which was fired by a single soldier. There were two basic types: the stick grenade (Stielhandgranate) and the egg grenade (Eihandgranate).

Stick hand grenade

Length	17.75 cm
Weight	0.2 kg
Fuse	A thin 0.2 kg pull-cord held in the shaft activated the bomb

The stick hand grenade had two parts. The head, which was shaped like a tin can, had a small projection at its base into which a fuse and the detonating cord were fitted. The second part of the grenade was the wooden shaft, at whose base was a screw-on alloy cap. The two parts were assembled once the fuse had been fitted. To throw the bomb, the base cap was unscrewed. The looped cord and a blue bead fell into the soldier's hand. When the cord was pulled, the fuse – with either a 4 or 9 second delay – was activated. A number

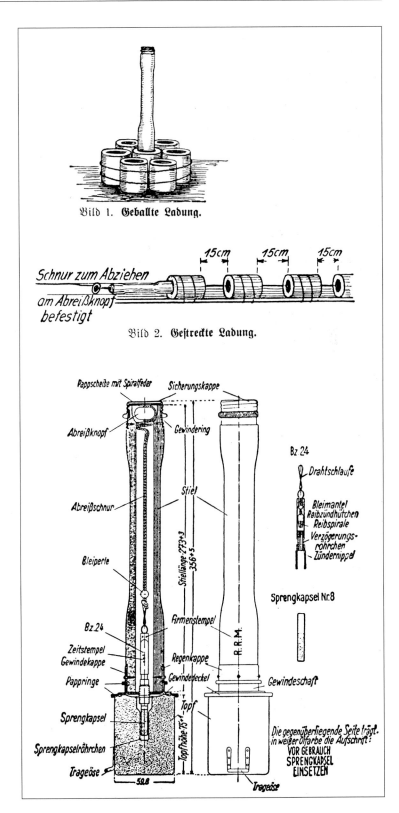

The stick hand grenade pattern 24, with its fuse (Bz 24), was a versatile weapon. With several heads fastened round a single complete grenade, it formed an explosive charge suitable for light demolitions. With a number of grenade heads fitted at intervals along a length of wood, the whole became a 'Bangalore Torpedo', which could be used to blow up barbed-wire obstructions.

of grenade heads could be fitted together to form a high-explosive charge called a *geballte Ladung*, which was placed against a target.

Alternatively, the heads could be pushed under barbed wire to act as a sort of 'Banagalore torpedo'.

Egg hand grenade
This lightweight bomb was also activated by unscrewing a cap fitted on the top of the grenade and pulling the cord which lay there.

THE 50 MM MORTAR
Weight   12.5 kg
Weight of bomb   1 kg
Maximum range   500 m
Method of firing By a spigot activated by a wheel at the side of the projector

81 MM MORTAR
This was the standard close-support mortar in the German service.

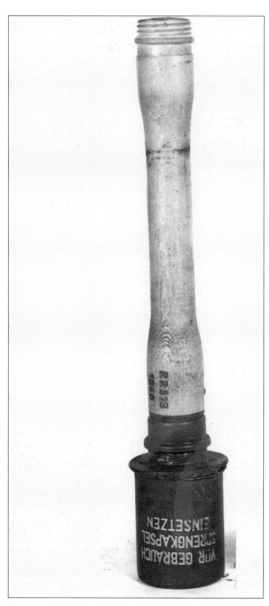

The standard hand grenade in the German service was the pattern 24. It had a head which was filled with explosive, and a wooden shaft inside which fitted the cord and fuse. When the cord was pulled, it activated a fuse which detonated the explosive after a pause of four seconds.

The 50 mm light mortar in action, Italy, 1944.

The two mortars on standard issue to German infantry units. On the left, the 81 mm piece which fired its bomb from a fixed firing pin, and on the right, the 50 mm mortar, which was operated by a wheel which activated a firing pin.

Total weight	28 kg
Weight of bomb	2.25 kg
Maximum traverse	10°
Elevation	47–88°
Maximum range	1,200 m

120 MM MORTAR 42

This was a German copy of the standard Russian mortar, but fitted with a wheeled cartridge. The range of this piece and the weight of the bomb it fired gave it power equivalent to a field howitzer.

Total weight	280 kg
Weight of shell	16 kg
Traverse	16°
Elevation	45–85°
Range	6,600 m

105 MM NEBELWERFER

This enlarged version of the 81 mm mortar was originally intended to fire smoke shells.

Total weight	105 kg
Traverse	13°
Elevation	45–80°
Range	3,300 m

The 120 mm mortar, here shown mounted on its wheeled carriage.

The Panzerwerfer 42 fired a salvo of ten 15 cm rockets from its mounting on a half-track.

The Nebelwerfer was a very effective weapon when used against infantry. It fired a pattern of six projectiles which screamed through the air, creating a nerve-shattering noise. Here the shells are being loaded into the barrels, from which they would be fired by electrical charge. Their discharge was accompanied by huge trails of fire and smoke.

The Panzerwerfer 42 was a motorized and upgunned version of the standard Nebelwerfer. Here, the ten 15 cm tubes of the Panzerwerfer 42 are being loaded.

15 CM NEBELWERFER 41

This six-barrelled rocket launcher entered service in 1942, and was a variant of the Russian multi-barrelled weapon which the German Army had encountered shortly after it invaded the Soviet Union.

The German Army version was fitted onto a 3.7 cm pak carriage, but could also be mounted on a half-track. It was served by a four-man crew.

The shells it fired were 2.5 kg in weight, and they could be projected over a range of 7,000 m. The weapon had the disadvantage that when fired, it raised huge clouds of smoke, and in flight each shell was accompanied by a smoke trail. An added advantage of the weapon was that the noise it made in flight was unnerving (it was known to the Allied armies as 'Moaning Minnie').

MINES

The Second World War witnessed a widespread use of land mines of both types. Mines which, at the outbreak of war, had been laid as single obstacles soon developed into belts of mines, and from that stage to mine fields and finally to 'mine marshes', which were vast areas of terrain sown with the devices.

With the extensive use of mines came the need to detect where the enemy had laid them, and this in turn led, on the part of the German Army, to developing mines made of glass, wood or concrete so as to avoid detection. German anti-personnel mines could be detonated by the weight of the human foot, whereas anti-tank mines only detonated under the greater pressure of a vehicle.

All mines, but particularly the anti-tank variety, could be fitted with anti-handling

Two SS grenadiers wait to go on a tank destruction mission. One carries a Teller mine which he will throw under the tracks of a tank to destroy it. Eastern Front, 1943.

devices which turned them into booby traps and, in addition, the principal anti-tank mine, the Teller, was used as a close-quarter weapon by soldiers, who either placed them on the outside of the enemy vehicles or else flung them under their tracks.

ANTI-PERSONNEL MINES

The device most feared by the Allied soldiers, and certainly the most lethal mine, was the S 35, which could be activated either by the pressure of a foot or by a trip wire. Less frequently, it was detonated by electrical charge.

When the S mine was fused to explode upon foot pressure, it was fitted with the Z 35 fuse, which required the weight of only 6.8 kg to activate. The fuse for a trip-wire device was of the pull variety, which could be fitted to take two or even three trip wires. The design of the S mine was two cylindrical-shaped metal casings fitted one inside the other. The outer case held a propellant charge and a 4½-second delay charge. When pressure was exerted, the propellant charge in the outer case flung the inner case into the air, at the same time operating the delay fuse. When this exploded, it flung out some 360 steel balls whose lethal range was 20 m but which could inflict injuries up to 100 m. The S 35 mine was 12.75 cm high and had a diameter of 10 cm. Its weight was 4 kg.

The S 44 mine was an improved version of the 35 pattern, and the improvement came in the way in which the 4½-second charge operated. As the mine was flung upwards, a release pin was pulled from the igniter and exploded the charge, which released the metal balls.

Being made of metal, the S mines were easily found by Allied metal detector teams, and it was for that reason that the mines were often fitted with booby trap and anti-handling devices.

The Schu 42 pattern mines worked on a very light pressure, and were frequently mixed in with anti-tank devices to prevent these from being detected and lifted. The body of the mine was of plywood or cardboard painted dull black and, when charged with explosive and fused, weighed just under 0.5 kg.

A slight pressure upon the lid of the mine activated the igniter by shearing through a holding pin, which released the striker, causing the mine to explode.

The 1943 pattern anti-personnel mine was similar in construction and design to the 42 pattern Schu mine, but its explosive filling was heavier at 1.5 kg.

There were other patterns of non-metallic mines, including the Type 42 wooden pattern, one made of glass and the pot mine. The German Army also used the Italian anti-personnel mine made of an early type of plastic known as Bakelite.

ANTI-TANK MINES

Of the forty types of anti-tank device, the standard German mine was the Teller. Four types of this weapon were those most commonly used. Their weight varied between 6 and 8.5 kg, and they were fitted with the Teller Mine 42 (15) pattern fuse.

The 42 pattern Teller mine was an updated version of the 35 type, and was cylindrical in shape and made of pressed steel. Its diameter was 32 cm. Situated centrally on the upper side of the mushroom-shaped lid was a detonator pocket. Because of its weight, the Teller mine was fitted with a carrying handle.

Two waterproofed sockets were fitted to hold the pull fuses, one in the side of the mine and the other in the base. A cylindrical socket on the top of the mine held the 15 cm diameter pressure-plate which consisted of a sealing ring and a strong spring which had to be depressed in order to activate the mine. In the centre of the plate was a socket for the igniter, a T Mi Z 42 (15) fuse.

The 5.5 kg explosive filling of the 42 pattern gave it a total weight of 8 kg.

When a pressure of more than 225 kg was exerted upon the pressure-plate, a hexagonal cap was forced down onto the head of the plunger, and this sheared the pin holding the striker which was located in the body of the igniter.

The 35 pattern Teller mine weighed 9.5 kg. The lid was fluted, and the pressure-plate extended across the whole mine. The standard T Mi Z 35 was used, but the mine could also take the 42 pattern igniter. The diameter of the mine was 32 cm, and the weight of its filling was 8.75 kg. In the case of the 35 pattern, the weight required to

The flame-thrower was a popular weapon in the German Army, but was also a dangerous one, for the team of two men were targets for enemy snipers. The men shown here are recruits to a pioneer unit, undergoing instruction on the weapon.

explode it was less than that of the 42 type – 80–180 kg.

There were earlier versions. The T Mi 29 detonated at a pressure of 45–125 kg, and was filled with a 4.5 kg explosive charge giving a total weight of 6 kg. The light anti-tank mine weighed 3.5 kg, of which 2.25 kg was the detonating charge. The diameter of the mine was 30.5 cm, and its height was 7.5 cm.

The Topf mine was one of the type designed to avoid detection, and was a hollow cylindrical disc of a plastic material, filled with explosive. The fuse was of a glass material, with an igniter made of a cardboard material.

The Riegel anti-tank mine was a box 80 cm long, within which was a tray holding 4 kg of Amatol explosive. The lid of the box rested on that charge, and pressure upon the lid sheared through two wires, pushing out the pins of the fuse, which caused the explosion.

The two principal fuses (Zünder) which armed the anti-tank mines were as follows:

T Mi Z 35

The Teller Mine Zünder 35 was used with trip wires to operate booby traps. It consisted of a brass body which held a sliding cylinder, a compressing spring, the striker and the striker spring. A variant of this fuse could be used either as a trip wire or designed to activate when the trip wire was cut.

T Mi Z 42

The Teller Mine Zünder 42 was a simple steel striker retained against the pressure of a steel spring by a shear wire.

CHAPTER SEVEN

THE PANZERS

INTRODUCTION

The military historian Matthew Cooper described the German Panzer arm of service as: 'a failure. A glorious failure . . . but a failure nonetheless . . . The significance of this failure was immense. The Panzer Divisions, the prime offensive weapon, had become indispensable . . . in both tactical and strategic terms . . . Upon the fortunes of the armoured force was based the fate of the whole army . . .'. He concluded that the fault for the demise of the Panzer arm lay in the hands of Hitler and the Army commanders, 'who failed to grasp the full implications of this new, revolutionary doctrine and consistently misused the force upon which their fortunes had come to depend'. Another reason was the neglect of equipment and organizational requirements, which stunted the Panzer arm's potential in the field.

Hitler was impressed by armour operating in conjunction with other arms. In 1933, after witnessing a demonstration of mobile troops, he had been very enthusiastic, although armoured theory and practice were not new in the Germany Army. Indeed, it would be true to say that Germany's armoured force was born on the steppes of Russia during the 1920s. Among other prohibitions, the conditions of the Versailles Treaty forbade the German Army from having armoured fighting vehicles. To circumvent this restriction, the governments of republican Germany and the Soviet Union entered into a conspiracy: the Soviet Union would grant a vast area of land upon which

The guidon of a Panzer unit being paraded through the streets of the unit's garrison town upon its return from active service.

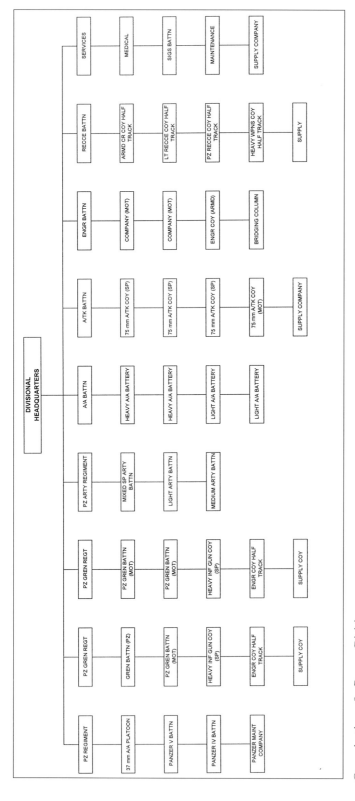

Organization of a Panzer Division.

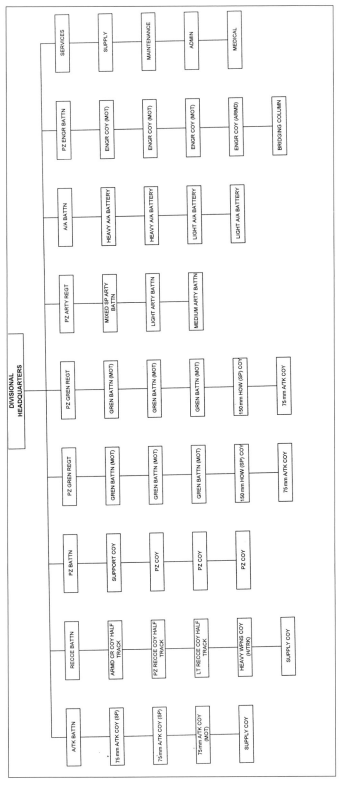

Organization of a Panzergrenadier Division.

In the years before Germany re-armed, motorized infantry training was carried out using light lorries. This vehicle is shown mounting a machine gun on the roof of the driver's cab.

the German military commanders could practice manoeuvres, while in another part of that territory, factories would be set up to construct the armoured fighting vehicles which German experts had designed and which the German commanders needed for their manoeuvres. A great number of German senior commanders and armour theorists went to Kasan in the Soviet Union and developed the skills required in handling armour in the mass and in conducting exercises using aircraft. Between them, the Army and Luftwaffe commanders evolved and developed the concept of Blitzkrieg.

This collaboration between Germany and Russia lasted until 1935, when the Nazi government withdrew the Panzer and Luftwaffe detachments from Soviet territory. Thereafter, it was on German soil that tank

design and construction was carried out. The first types of Panzer had been given the cover name 'agricultural tractors', to hoodwink the officers of the Armistice Commission, and because that name fitted in with conventional German military thinking that armoured vehicles would be used principally to bring supplies forward across the broken and difficult terrain of the battlefield. This negative attitude towards the strategic employment of armour as a separate arm of service was common to many generals of the high command: one even went so far as to say: 'The idea of Panzer divisions is Utopian.' But the protagonists advanced their ideas, and a Mechanized Troops Inspectorate was set up in June 1934. Hitler's repudiation of the Treaty of Versailles brought the expansion of the German Army, and with it

In the years before Germany re-armed, the Army used dummy tanks on manoeuvres. This photo shows a group of wooden dummies carried by their crews.

Dummy tanks collaborating with infantry on manoeuvres.

In the years during which the German Army was forbidden to have armoured fighting vehicles, the codename given to such machines was 'Industrial Tractor'. This industrial tractor is towing an artillery piece.

the beginning of an armoured force. As early as July 1935, an *ad hoc* Panzer division successfully carried out a training exercise which demonstrated that the movement – and more particularly, the control – of major Panzer units was practicable. Even further than that, a general staff exercise had studied the employment of a whole Panzer corps in action. The year 1935 also saw the birth of a new arm of service when the Armoured Troops Command was created, which was followed by the raising of the first three Panzer divisions. The Armoured Troops Command had, as yet, no real authority, for armour was not considered to be an equal partner with the infantry, cavalry and artillery arms.

General Guderian was given the post of Chief of Mobile Troops, and took over the development and training of the entire mechanized force of the Army. As a consequence, he had direct access to Hitler. During 1938, two more Panzer divisions were created, as well as a command structure which allowed the Panzer arm – in theory, at

least – to be one of the partners in the Field Army.

It was one thing to be accepted as a partner, it was another to be equipped for that role. The Panzers which the armoured divisions needed were issued to non-Panzer units, and another hindrance was that tank quality was poor. The majority of machines in the armoured force were Panzer I and II types, which were not only obsolete, but were under-gunned and under-armoured. A third negative factor was the raising of three light (mobile) divisions in November 1938. These, together with a fourth division, were created instead of Panzer divisions.

It was not until 1940 that the OKW placed all German armour within the framework of its Panzer divisions. This favourable situation was of brief duration, for by the middle years of the war one-fifth of the AFV strengths still remained outside a divisional framework. One final factor was that the German leadership neglected to plan for new types of replacement tanks. Apart from the existing III and IV types, no preparation was made to produce adequate

These officers are the men who pioneered the art of Blitzkrieg or ('lightning war'). The seated figure on the left is General Nehring, the Panzer theorist, and the non-uniformed figure seated in the front rank is Guderian.

stocks of tanks or other armoured vehicles or any new marks of Panzer. It was not until 1943 that top priority was given to AFV production. Total production of Panzers in the second month of the war, September 1939, was only fifty-seven machines. Clearly, there was a need for improvement.

German superiority in the matter of Panzer operations during the war owed nothing to the number or quality of the machines it fielded, but was rather the product of superior organizations and training. The campaign in Poland did not see the Panzer force being used in the way that Guderian and the other theorists had planned. It was, instead, the speed with which the whole German Army moved – not just that of the Panzer divisions – which brought victory. For the Polish campaign, the German Army had fielded 2,100 tanks, and lost 218 of them. More serious than the 10 per cent battle loss was the high rate of mechanical failure, which kept 25 per cent of the machines out of action at any one time. There had been no improvement by 1940, when the war in the west opened. For that campaign, out of a total of 2,574 machines, fewer than 627 were of the heavier Panzer III and Panzer IV types, and 1,613 were the obsolete Panzer I and II. Nevertheless, as Guderian recorded, the Panzer force fought its battle more or less without interference from the OKW, and as a result, achieved dramatic successes.

One of the few examples of Hitler's direct interference was when he halted the Panzer divisions outside Dunkirk, an act which allowed Britain to withdraw the bulk of its Army.

As a result of the experiences gained through the victory in the west, it became clear that the Panzer arm of service would soon rise to become a partner equal to the infantry. Hitler was determined to invade the Soviet Union, but needed to increase the number of Panzer divisions. To achieve that growth, he could have decided to increase the output of German tank factories. Instead, he deluded himself that numbers equalled strength, and raised the number of armoured divisions from 10 to 21 by the simple expedient of halving the AFV strength of each division. Thus, each division was made up of a single tank regiment numbering 150–200 machines. Hitler was convinced that a Panzer division fielding a single armoured regiment had the striking power of a division which fielded two regiments. It was a fatal mistake, particularly since Panzer production in the first six months of 1941 averaged only 212 vehicles per month. The total number of machines available for the new war against Russia was 5,262, of which only 4,198 were held to be 'front-line' Panzers, and of that total, only 1,404 were the better-armed Panzer III and IV. Those vehicles, good as they were, were soon to be confronted by the Red Army's superior T 34s and KV Is. Although inferior in every respect, the Panzer IIIs and IVs were forced to remain in front-line service until the Panzer V (Panther) and the Panzer VI (Tiger) types could be rushed into service. An example of the blindness of the general staff towards armour requirements was shown by General Halder, who seemed to be satisfied that 431 new Panzers would be produced by the end of July 1941, although this was less than half the number of machines lost during that period. Throughout the war, replacements never equalled the losses suffered.

To summarize: German industry was not equipped for the mass production of AFVs, and the ones which were produced for the Army were inferior to those of its opponents – certainly until the Panther and the Tiger came into service. Although the Panzer arm fought valiantly to the end, from 1943 it was firmly on the defensive, except for a few isolated offensives. The greatest mistake was that the supreme commander, Hitler, would accept no limitations upon his strategic plans, and sent major armoured formations across vast areas of country without consideration for the strain upon crews or machines and the drain upon the petrol resources of the Reich, and then committed those tired crews and worn-out vehicles to battle against unequal odds. Because of those and many other factors, Matthew Cooper must be seen as correct in his verdict that the Panzer arm was a failure.

THE PANZERS

The Panzer divisions of the German Army were eventually numbered 1–27, 116, 232 and 233. The establishment also contained named Panzer divisions, as well as light divisions, which were later upgraded to Panzer status. When general mobilization was ordered, the Army had five Panzer and four light divisions on establishment.

The infantry component of the 1st Panzer Division was Schützen Regiment No. 1, made up of two battalions, each of five companies; the 2nd Panzer Division incorporated the 2nd Schützen Regiment, with two battalions, each of five companies; the 3rd Panzer Division had the 3rd Schützen Regiment, also with two battalions, each of five companies; the 4th Panzer Division's infantry component was the 12th Schützen Regiment, with two battalions, each of four companies; and the 5th Panzer Division had the 13th Schützen Regiment, with two battalions, each of four companies.

The organization of the light divisions was not standard. The 1st Light Division had

The motorcycle reconnaissance company of an SS regiment, Poland, 1939.

Cavalry Schützen Regiment No. 4, which was reorganized into a motorized infantry brigade, with a single infantry regiment, a recce battalion and a tank regiment. The 2nd Light Division had Cavalry Schützen Regiments Nos 6 and 7, formed into two motorized infantry regiments, a recce regiment and a battalion of tanks; the infantry regiments were made up of two battalions, each of which fielded four squadrons. The 3rd Light Division had Cavalry Schützen Regiment No. 8 on establishment, formed into a motorized infantry regiment of two battalions, each fielding two squadrons; the divisional establishment was completed with a motorcycle battalion and a Panzer battalion. The 4th Light Division fielded Cavalry Schützen Regiments Nos 10 and 11, forming two motorized infantry regiments and a Panzer battalion; each of the motorized regiments was composed of two battalions, both of these fielding four squadrons.

In the months between the end of the Polish campaign and the opening of the war in the west, the four light divisions were upgraded to Panzer division status, and were numbered 6–9. Three motorized infantry regiments were taken to create the 10th Panzer Division. Other infantry regiments were used to increase the strength of the first three Schützen regiments to three battalions, as well as helping to create the 11th Schützen Regiment.

The number of Panzer divisions on establishment was increased from 10 to 20 during the autumn of 1940, and that number was further increased during 1941, with the 21st Panzer Division being raised for service in Africa. During the winter of 1941/2, Panzer divisions Nos 22, 23 and 24 were raised. The 24th was created by conversion of the 1st Cavalry Division, whose mounted regiments were renamed and renumbered Schützen Regiments Nos 21 and 26.

Members of an SS reconnaissance company,
France, 1940.

On 5 July 1942, the Schützen regiments of
Panzer divisions were renamed Panzergrenadier regiments, and there was a change
in organization, with the disbandment of the
machine gun company which had been on
the strength of each battalion. Panzer
Divisions Nos 25, 26 and 27 were formed
during 1942. Ten divisions were destroyed on
the Eastern Front and in Africa, the 14th,
16th and 24th were lost at Stalingrad, while
the 22nd and 27th suffered such severe losses
that they had to be broken up. The 14th,
16th and 24th Divisions were then re-raised
in France. In Tunisia, the 10th, 15th and 21st
Panzer Divisions were lost, as were the 90th
Light Division and the 164th and 999th Light
Africa Divisions. The 15th and 90th Light
were re-raised as Panzergrenadier divisions.

The 21st Panzer was also re-raised in its
former role. Neither the 164th Light nor the
999th Light were re-formed.

Most of the Panzer divisions on establishment were reorganized along the lines of a
'Panzer Division 1943 Pattern'. In this, the
first battalion of each division became
armoured Panzergrenadiers, able to fight
from their armoured vehicles. The first three
companies of the battalion had a war
establishment of 4 heavy and 39 light
machine guns, 2 medium mortars, and
7.5 cm and 3.7 cm guns. No. 4 Company had
three heavy PAK, 2 light infantry guns, six
7.5 cm and 21 machine guns.

The first, second and third companies of
the battalions in the new-pattern division
each had 4 heavy machine guns, 18 light
machines guns and 2 medium mortars. No. 4
Company had 4 heavy mortars, 3 heavy PAK
and 3 machine guns. No. 9 – the infantry gun
company – had 6 guns mounted on tracks.
No. 10 Company was the pioneer company,
and was equipped with 12 machine guns and
18 flame-throwers.

During 1943/4, the 18th Panzer Division was
broken up, and units were taken from it to
create the 18th Artillery Division. During this
period the 'Panzer Lehr' Division was raised,
and three reserve Panzer divisions were used to
create the 9th, 11th and 116th Panzer Divisions.
The military disasters of the summer of 1944
brought about the creation of Panzer Brigades
101–113, which were used to reinforce Panzer
or Panzergrenadier divisions which had
suffered heavy losses. During the autumn of
1944, the Army followed the pattern of the SS
in combining two Panzer divisions into a
permanent corps structure. Until that time,
Army Panzer Corps HQs had been administrative units, to which divisions had been
allocated as required. Army Panzer corps were
then created, and 'Großdeutschland',
'Feldherrenhalle' and XXIV Panzer Corps were
created. The first named contained the

'Großdeutschland' Panzergrenadier Division, the Panzergrenadier Division 'Brandenburg' and the 'Großdeutschland' Musketier Regiment. The 'Feldherrnhalle' Corps had 1st and 2nd Divisions of that name, and the XXIV Panzer Corps contained the 16th and 17th Panzer Divisions, as well as the 29th Panzer Fusilier Regiment.

The final reorganization of the Panzer arm of service saw the creation of the 'Panzer Division 1945'. This was an internal rearrangement which created and fielded a Panzer battle group because there was insufficient fuel to move all the Panzer vehicles, and only the machine gun company and the heavy weapons company were mobile.

PANZER DIVISIONS OF THE ARMY

1ST PANZER DIVISION

Raised during October 1935, it fought in Poland, on the Western Front and in Russia. During 1943 it was posted to France, and then to the Balkans, before returning to the Eastern Front. After a fighting retreat, it ended the war in Austria, where it surrendered to the British.

Composition

Panzer Regiment No. 1, Panzergrenadier Regiments Nos 1 and 113

2ND PANZER DIVISION

Formed in October 1935, the 2nd fought in Poland, in France, in the Balkans and on the Eastern Front. Moved to France in January 1944, the division fought in Normandy, and later in the Ardennes. It surrendered at the end of the war in Plauen.

Composition

Panzer Regiment No. 3, Panzergrenadier Regiments Nos 2 and 304

3RD PANZER DIVISION

Raised during October 1935, it fought in Poland, in Belgium, France and in the Soviet Union. During the German Army's withdrawal battles of 1944, the 3rd was in action in Hungary before surrendering in eastern Austria.

Composition

Panzer Regiment No. 6, Panzergrenadier Regiments Nos 3 and 394

4TH PANZER DIVISION

Raised in 1938, it served in Poland and in France before going on to the Eastern Front. It was involved in the retreat through Latvia during the autumn of 1944, and after fighting in the Courland battles, the 4th withdrew into Germany, where the remnant of the division surrendered to the Americans.

Composition

Panzer Regiment No. 35, Panzergrenadier Regiments Nos 12 and 33

5TH PANZER DIVISION

Raised during November 1938, it fought in Poland, in the west, the Balkans and on the Eastern Front. Late in 1944 it fought in the Courland battles, where it lost heavily. The remnant of the division surrendered to the Soviets.

Composition

Panzer Regiment No. 31, Panzergrenadier Regiments Nos 13 and 14

6TH PANZER DIVISION

One of the series of Panzer formations raised shortly after the outbreak of war in 1939, it was created out of the 1st Light Division. The 6th served during the campaign in France, and was then moved to the Eastern Front. During May 1942 it was refitted, and returned to Russia in December of that year. Posted to Hungary, the 6th withdrew into Czechoslovakia, where its remnants surrendered.

Composition
Panzer Regiment No. 11, Panzergrenadier Regiments Nos 4 and 114

7TH PANZER DIVISION

The 7th was formed out of the 2nd Light Division during October 1939, and served in France and later on the Eastern Front. Late in the war, it fought in the Baltic states until forced to withdraw westwards under the pressure of the Red Army.

Composition
Panzer Regiment No. 25, Panzergrenadier Regiments Nos. 6 and 7

8TH PANZER DIVISION

Raised during October 1939 out of the 3rd Light Division, it fought in France, in the Balkans and on the Eastern Front. In 1944, while fighting with Army Group South, it withdrew first into the Carpathian Mountains, then into Moravia, where it surrendered in May 1945.

Composition
Panzer Regiment No. 10, Panzergrenadier Regiments Nos. 8 and 28

9TH PANZER DIVISION

Raised during January 1940 out of the 4th Light Division, the 9th saw action on the Western Front, the Balkans and finally Russia. Removed to France during March 1944, it fought in Normandy, and later in the Ardennes. Its remnant surrendered in the Ruhr pocket during April 1945.

Composition
Panzer Regiment No. 33, Panzergrenadier Regiments Nos 10 and 11

10TH PANZER DIVISION

Raised in Prague during April 1939, elements of the division fought in the campaign against Poland as part of 'Kempf's Panzer Formation'. Then followed action in France during 1940, and subsequently in Soviet Russia. Posted back to France, it was part of the force which countered the Canadian raid on Dieppe during August 1942. In December 1942, it was transported to Tunisia, where it was destroyed in May 1943. Unusually for a German formation, the 10th was never re-raised.

Composition
Panzer Regiment No. 7, Panzergrenadier Regiments Nos 69 and 86

11TH PANZER DIVISION

The 11th was created during August 1940, around units from the 5th Panzer Division. It fought in Russia, and remained there until June 1944, when it was posted to the south of France for refitting. There, it saw action in late 1944 against the invading American and French forces. During the course of a long fighting retreat, the 11th withdrew into the Saar and thence into Bavaria, where it surrendered.

Composition
Panzer Regiment No. 15, Panzergrenadier Regiments Nos 110 and 111

12TH PANZER DIVISION

Created in October 1940 out of the 2nd Motorized Division, it was first employed in Russia. It then fought in the Courland battles before surrendering to the Soviet forces in May 1945.

Composition
Panzer Regiment No. 29, Panzergrenadier Regiments Nos 5 and 25

13TH PANZER DIVISION

Formed in Romania during October 1940, the 13th fought in Russia until autumn 1944, when it was posted to Hungary. It was totally destroyed in the fighting for Budapest during January 1945, but was immediately reconstituted as Panzer Division 'Feldherrenhalle' No. 2.

Composition
Panzer Regiment No. 4, Panzergrenadier Regiments Nos 66 and 93

14TH PANZER DIVISION
Originally the 4th Infantry Division, it was converted to Panzer status in the summer of 1940. It fought in the Jugoslavian campaign, and then on the Eastern Front. Destroyed in the Battle of Stalingrad, the 14th was re-formed during the summer of 1943, and returned to Russia, where it was again almost totally destroyed. Transferred to Courland, its remnant surrendered to the Russians.

Composition
Panzer Regiment No. 36, Panzergrenadier Regiments Nos 103 and 108

15TH PANZER DIVISION
The 15th was created out of units of the 10th Panzer Division during August 1940, and retitled the 15th Light Division when it was posted to Libya in April 1941. It was later reorganized as a Panzer division, and at the end of the war in Africa, it surrendered in Tunisia. The 15th was re-formed in July 1943 as a Panzergrenadier division.

Composition
Panzer Regiment No. 8, Panzergrenadier Regiments Nos 115 and 200

16TH PANZER DIVISION
Originally an infantry division, the 16th fought in Russia, and was destroyed at Stalingrad in February 1943. It was immediately re-formed in France, and was posted to Italy. In November 1943, it returned to the Eastern Front, where its remnant surrendered in May 1945.

Composition
Panzer Regiment No. 2, Panzergrenadier Regiments Nos 64 and 79

17TH PANZER DIVISION
Raised in October 1940, it was posted to Russia, where it was destroyed in April 1945.

Composition
Panzer Regiment No. 39, Panzergrenadier Regiments Nos 40 and 63

18TH PANZER DIVISION
Raised in October 1940, the division saw action on the Eastern Front, where it suffered heavy losses and was regrouped.

Composition
Panzer Regiment No. 27, Panzergrenadier Regiments Nos 52 and 101

19TH PANZER DIVISION
Created in October 1940, it fought on the Eastern Front. When the German Army withdrew from Russia, the 19th's line of retreat took it through the Ukraine and into East Prussia. There, it was forced to retreat once again, this time into Bohemia, where its remnant ended the war.

Composition
Panzer Regiment No. 27, Panzergrenadier Regiments Nos 73 and 74

20TH PANZER DIVISION
Formed in October 1940, it fought on the Eastern Front until it was posted to Romania during August 1944. In December of that year, it fought in Hungary, where it passed into Russian captivity.

Composition
Panzer Regiment No. 21, Panzergrenadier Regiments Nos 59 and 112

Infantry often used Panzers as carriers: a dangerous tactic when the tank's main armament was fired. Here the infantry are returning enemy fire. Russia, autumn 1941.

A German column under fire in the first winter on the Eastern Front. One soldier is firing his rifle using his comrade's shoulder to steady his aim, while a third soldier observes the effect of the fire.

21ST PANZER DIVISION

Raised during February 1941 as the 5th Light Division, it was sent to Libya, where it was restructured as a Panzer division during July of that year. It fought in Africa until the Axis Armies surrendered in May 1943. In July of that year it was re-raised in France, and served on the Western Front until January 1945, when it was posted to the Eastern Front.

Composition

In the African campaign: Panzer Regiment No. 5, Motorized Infantry Regiments Nos 104 and Panzergrenadier Regiment No. 492; in north-west Europe: Panzer Regiment No. 22, Panzergrenadier Regiments Nos 125 and 192

22ND PANZER DIVISION

Created during September 1941, the 22nd served on the Eastern Front, where it was almost totally destroyed. Elements of the division were taken to help form the 27th Panzer Division in September 1942. The 22nd was eventually disbanded.

23RD PANZER DIVISION

It was the original intention to raise the 23rd in October 1940, but this was delayed, and it was not until September 1941 that the division was concentrated. During March 1942 it was posted to the Eastern Front. At the end of 1943, after it had suffered heavy losses, it withdrew into Poland, and fought there until September 1944, when it was posted to Hungary.

Composition

Panzer Regiment No. 201, Panzergrenadier Regiments Nos 126 and 128

24TH PANZER DIVISION

This formation was created during February 1942, with the greatest part of its effectives being supplied by the 1st Cavalry Division. The 24th was destroyed at Stalingrad, but was re-formed and posted to Italy before returning to Russia. It was then posted to Hungary and Slovakia. In January 1945, the 24th, now in West Prussia, retreated into Schleswig-Holstein, where it surrendered in May.

Composition

Panzer Regiment No. 24, Panzergrenadier Regiments Nos 21 and 26

27TH PANZER DIVISION

The first moves to create this division were made during 1942, but before it was completely raised, the 27th had been posted to the Eastern Front. It was destroyed during January 1943.

28TH PANZER DIVISION

This division was created during April 1944, out of the 17th Reserve Panzer Division and the 16th Panzer Grenadier Division. It fought on the Western Front, and its remnant surrendered in the Ruhr pocket in April 1945.

PANZER LEHR DIVISION

This formation was raised during November 1943 out of demonstration units of Panzer training schools. It fought on the Western Front from June 1944 until it surrendered in the Ruhr pocket in April 1945.

Composition

Panzer Regiment No. 130, Panzergrenadier Regiments Nos 901 and 902

Towards the end of the war a number of Panzer divisions were raised, but these were divisions in name only. They included the formations numbered 232 and 233, and the named Panzer divisions 'Norway', 'Kurmark', 'Holstein', 'Jüterbog' and 'Münchenberg'.

Included in the roll of Panzer divisions are the Panzer Para Division 'Hermann Goering' and 'Großdeutschland'. These eventually rose to corps strength, and are included in the list of Panzer corps.

The regimental standard of the SS 'Leibstandarte Adolf Hitler'. The colours carried by SS units were different in shape from those carried by the Army.

PANZER DIVISIONS OF THE WAFFEN-SS

1ST SS PANZER DIVISION 'LEIBSTANDARTE ADOLF HITLER'

'Leibstandarte Adolf Hitler' rose from a bodyguard unit, through motorized infantry status, to that of a motorized division in June 1941, a Panzergrenadier division in December 1942, and finally, a Panzer division. In one of those roles, it fought on every European front from Poland in 1939 to Vienna in 1945, and took a distinctive part in the Battle of Kursk in July 1943.

Composition as a Panzer division
SS Panzer Regiment No. 1, Panzergrenadier Regiments Nos 1 and 2

2ND SS PANZER DIVISION 'DAS REICH'

'Das Reich' grew out of the SS regiments which were grouped as the SS Verfügungs-truppen division in the first year of the war. The division fought in every European

Panzergrenadiers of 'Das Reich' SS Division, sweeping forward to recapture the city of Kharkov, 1943.

The Pioneer Company of the 'Das Reich' Division is here seen ferrying units of the division across the River Beresina, Eastern Front, July 1941.

campaign of the Second World War, rising from a unit in regimental strength to that of a Panzer division by October 1943.

Composition as a Panzer division
SS Panzer Regiment No. 2, Panzergrenadier Regiments Nos 3 and 4

3RD SS PANZER DIVISION 'TOTENKOPF'
'Totenkopf' was formed around concentration camp units and other units of the 'Verfügungs Truppen Division'. It fought as a motorized infantry, then as a Panzergrenadier formation before being raised to the status of a full Panzer division in October 1943. 'Totenkopf' fought on both the Eastern and Western Fronts, and finished the war in Austria and Czechoslovakia.

Composition as a Panzer division
SS Panzer Regiment No. 3, Panzergrenadier Regiments Nos 5 and 6

5TH SS PANZER DIVISION 'WIKING'
'Wiking' ('Viking') was raised around a cadre of Dutch, Flemish, Danish and Norwegian volunteers during December 1940. It served on the Eastern Front, rising through motorized status to that of a Panzergrenadier division, finally becoming a Panzer division in October 1943. It finished the war in Austria and Czechoslovakia.

Composition as a Panzer division
SS Panzer Regiment No. 5, Panzergrenadier Regiments Nos 9 and 10

Soldiers of the SS Panzer division 'Das Reich', here seen moving out of the line after being relieved. They are wearing camouflage shirts.

The motorcycle detachment of the reconnaissance battalion of the SS 'Das Reich' Regiment, Poland, 1939.

Grenadiers of the 'Hitler Youth' Panzer Division searching the skies for Allied aircraft, Normandy, 1944. The machine gun is the M 3.

9TH SS PANZER DIVISION 'HOHENSTAUFEN'

'Hohenstaufen' was raised as a Panzergrenadier formation, and in February 1944 was upgraded to the status of a Panzer division. It fought on both the Eastern and Western Fronts, notably in Normandy, at Arnhem and in the Battle of the Bulge before returning to the Eastern Front and to Hungary, where it was practically destroyed. Its remnant surrendered to the Russians in May 1945.

Composition as a Panzer division

Panzer Regiment No. 9, Panzergrenadier Regiments Nos 19 and 20

10TH SS PANZER DIVISION 'FRUNDSBERG'

The 10th was raised as a Panzergrenadier formation, and was upgraded to the status of a Panzer division in October 1943. It fought on both the Eastern and Western Fronts, was in Normandy, in the fighting for Arnhem, and in the battle for Strasburg. On return from the Western to the Eastern Front, it was encircled and almost destroyed. It surrendered to the Red Army at the end of the war.

Composition as a Panzer division

Panzer Regiment No. 10, Panzergrenadier Regiments Nos 21 and 22

12TH SS PANZER DIVISION 'HITLER JUGEND'

It was raised as a Panzergrenadier division in July 1943, and attained the status of a Panzer division during October of that year. The division's first action was in Normandy, and it served on the Western Front until February 1945, when it was posted to Hungary. The division fought its way westwards into Austria, and surrendered to the American forces at the end of the war.

Composition as a Panzer division

Panzer Regiment No. 12, Panzergrenadier Regiments Nos 25 and 26

PANZERGRENADIER DIVISIONS OF THE ARMY

The infantry regiments which in 1937 formed the first lorried infantry formations bore the title 'Rifle' (Schützen). That was changed in March 1943, when the Schützen regiments were renamed 'Panzergrenadier'. Although the Schützen formations had originally formed part of the infantry establishment, I have included them here, within the Panzer arm of service.

2ND INFANTRY DIVISION (MOTORIZED)

This formation was raised in 1934. As a motorized division, it fought in Poland in 1939 and on the Western Front in 1940. In December 1940, it was reorganized into the 12th Panzer Division.

Composition

Panzer Regiment No. 29, Panzergrenadier Regiments Nos 110 and 111

3RD INFANTRY DIVISION (MOTORIZED)

Formed in October 1940 by conversion of the 3rd Infantry Division, it fought on the Eastern Front from the start of the war against Russia, and was destroyed in Stalingrad. The division was re-created two months later, and from September 1944 it served on the Western Front.

A Panzergrenadier battalion opens an armoured attack on the Eastern Front.

Anti-tank gunners of the SS 'Hitler Youth' firing their weapon in the fighting around Falaise.

Composition

Panzer Battalion No. 103, Panzergrenadier Regiments Nos 8 and 29

5TH LIGHT (AFRICA) DIVISION

It was raised in January 1941, and was posted to Libya, where it was a component of the Africa corps. In July 1941, the 5th Light was re-formed and retitled the 21st Panzer Division.

Composition as a Panzer division

Panzer Regiment No. 5, Panzergrenadier Regiments Nos 192 and 492

10TH INFANTRY DIVISION (MOTORIZED)

Created out of the 10th Infantry Division during October 1940, the 10th served on the Eastern Front from June 1941 until the end of the war. Reduced in strength by severe losses, it was amalgamated with a reserve Panzer division in March 1944, but the amalgamated formation retained the designation 10th.

Composition

Panzer Battalion No. 110, Panzergrenadier Regiments Nos 20 and 41

13TH INFANTRY DIVISION (MOTORIZED)

This division was converted from infantry to motorized status in 1937, and fought in Poland and then on the Western Front. In October of that year it was reorganized into the 13th Panzer Division.

Composition as a Panzer division

Panzer Regiment No. 4, Panzergrenadier Regiments Nos 66 and 93

14TH INFANTRY DIVISION (MOTORIZED)

Raised as an infantry formation, it fought as such in Poland and on the Western Front. During October 1940, it converted to the status of a motorized division, and it served on the Eastern Front from June 1941. During the summer of 1943 it reverted back to infantry status.

Composition

Panzer Battalion No. 114, Panzergrenadier Regiments Nos 11 and 53

15TH PANZERGRENADIER DIVISION

In May 1943, the 15th Panzer Division surrendered in North Africa, and from the remnant which had escaped captivity and had reached Sicily, a Panzergrenadier division was created. This then fought as part of the German 10th Army, which was defending the Tyrrhenian side of the Italian peninsula. During the early autumn of 1944, the 15th was transferred to France, and participated in the Battle of the Bulge and then in the defence of the Reichswald.

Composition

Panzer Battalion No. 115, Panzergrenadier Regiments Nos 104 and 115

16TH INFANTRY DIVISION (MOTORIZED)

Formed during October 1940 from an amalgamation of two other infantry units, it fought in Jugoslavia and then the Eastern Front, where it was upgraded to Panzergrenadier status. In March 1944, it was destroyed in the fighting in the Ukraine, but the remnant was not re-formed as the 16th Panzergrenadier Division, but was embodied into the 116th Panzer Division.

Composition

Panzer Battalion No. 116, Panzergrenadier Regiments Nos 60 and 156

18TH INFANTRY DIVISION (MOTORIZED)

Raised in October 1940 from the 18th Infantry Division, as a motorized formation it served in Jugoslavia and the Eastern Front, where it was destroyed during July 1944. Re-formed, initially as a battle group, the formation was involved in the bitter fighting at the approaches to East Prussia. Decimated once again, the 18th was re-formed, put into action and again destroyed. Re-formed and put into the battle around Berlin, it was destroyed for a fourth time.

Composition

Panzer Battalion No. 118, Panzergrenadier Regiments Nos 30 and 51

20TH INFANTRY DIVISION (MOTORIZED)

Raised in October 1934 as the 20th Infantry Division, it was motorized in 1937. Serving in Poland and on the Western Front, it was selected to take part in Operation SEA LION, the aborted invasion of the British Isles. During its period in combat on the Eastern Front, it was converted to Panzergrenadier status.

Composition

Panzer Battalion No. 120, Panzergrenadier Regiments Nos 76 and 90

25TH INFANTRY DIVISION (MOTORIZED)

Formed in October 1940 from the 25th Infantry Division, it fought on the Eastern Front. It was destroyed during July 1944, re-formed in December 1944, and returned to action in February 1945.

Composition

Panzer Battalion No. 125, Panzergrenadier Regiments Nos 35 and 119

29TH INFANTRY DIVISION (MOTORIZED)

Formed in 1937, it fought in Poland, on the Western Front and in Russia. Destroyed at Stalingrad in January 1943, it was re-created and posted to the South-Western Front in Italy.

Composition

Panzer Battalion No. 129, Panzergrenadier Regiments Nos 15 and 71

36TH INFANTRY DIVISION (MOTORIZED)

Created from the 36th Infantry Division, it fought on the Russian Front until the summer of 1943, when it reverted back to being a standard infantry division.

Composition

Panzer Battalion No. 136, Panzergrenadier Regiments Nos 87 and 118

60TH INFANTRY DIVISION (MOTORIZED)

Created from the 60th Infantry Division, it fought in the Balkan campaign and then the Eastern Front, where it was destroyed at Stalingrad. Re-created in June 1943, it was given a new title, Panzergrenadier Division 'Feldherrenhalle'. On return to the Eastern Front, it was again destroyed in July 1944. Re-formed for a second time during August, it returned to Russia in October. In the following month it was upgraded in status to become Panzer Division 'Feldherrenhalle'.

Composition as a Panzergrenadier division

Panzer Battalion No. 160, Fusilier Regiment 'Feldherrenhalle' No. 120 and Grenadier Regiment 'Feldherrenhalle' No. 271

90TH LIGHT (AFRICA) DIVISION

Created in August 1941, it was renamed the 90th Infantry Division (Motorized) in March 1942. It fought in North Africa until it was destroyed in May 1943.

Composition

Panzer Battalion No. 190, Panzergrenadier Regiments Nos 155 and 200

164TH LIGHT (AFRICA) DIVISION

The 164th was raised around units from 'Fortress Crete', and posted to North Africa, where it fought until destroyed in May 1943.

Composition

Panzer Battalion No. 164, Panzergrenadier Regiments Nos 125 and 382

386TH INFANTRY DIVISION (MOTORIZED)

This unit was formed at the end of 1942 as a standard infantry unit, and in March 1943 was upgraded to the status of a motorized division. When the 3rd Panzer Division was destroyed, draftees from the 386th were taken to re-create the 3rd Panzer Division. The 386th was then stood down.

Composition as an infantry formation

Panzergrenadier Regiments Nos 149 and 153

PANZERGRENADIER DIVISION 'BRANDENBURG'

The origins of this division lay with units created by the German counter-intelligence formation 'Die Abwehr'. Downgraded to a standard Panzergrenadier formation, those Abwehr groups were joined by others taken from 'Fortress Division Rhodes'. 'Brandenburg' fought on the Eastern Front, and in December 1944 was amalgamated with Panzergrenadier Division 'Großdeutschland' to form Panzer Corps 'Großdeutschland', although it retained its own name.

Composition

In 1943: 1st, 2nd, 3rd and 4th Regiments; in 1945: 1st and 2nd Jäger Regiments, Panzer Group 'Wietersheim'.

PANZERGRENADIER DIVISION 'KURMARK'

Formed in February 1943, this formation spent its whole life on the Eastern Front.

PANZERGRENADIER DIVISION 'GROßDEUTSCHLAND'

The original motorized infantry regiment 'Großdeutschland' was upgraded to divisional status during May 1942. As an elite unit serving on the Eastern Front, it was frequently moved from one threatened sector to another, and as a consequence fought with several army groups. After a regrouping of its units in East Prussia in December 1944, the formation stayed in that province and defended it until it was overrun at the end of March 1945. Prior to this, in December 1944, 'Großdeutschland' had combined with the 'Brandenburg' Division to form the Panzer Corps 'Großdeutschland'.

Composition

Panzer Regiment 'Großdeutschland', Grenadier Regiment 'Großdeutschland' and Fusilier Regiment 'Großdeutschland'

PANZER DIVISION 'HERMANN GOERING'

This formation was created as a brigade in the summer of 1942, from the 'Hermann Goering' Regiment. In January 1943 it underwent conversion to the status of a Panzer division. Destroyed in Tunisia, it was re-formed in June 1943, and served chiefly in the Italian Theatre of Operations.

Composition

Panzer Regiment 'Hermann Goering', 'Hermann Goering' Grenadier Regiments Nos 1 and 2, Jäger Regiment 'Hermann Goering'

PANZERGRENADIER DIVISIONS OF THE WAFFEN-SS

4TH SS POLICE PANZERGRENADIER DIVISION

This was created on 18 September 1939, on the direct order of Adolf Hitler. The personnel of the infantry (later Grenadier) regiments were members of the state police forces reinforced with units of the Army. The 4th fought in the campaign in France and Flanders, and went on to serve in the Army of Occupation until it left to fight on the Eastern Front. Casualties reduced it to a battle group during September 1943, but in June 1944, a new division was created. This was then sent to the Balkans on anti-partisan operations, and during January 1945 it fought in Pomerania and in Mecklenburg. It fought its way to the Elbe, and there passed into American captivity.

Composition

Police Rifle (Schützen) Regiments Nos 1, 2 and 3

11TH SS VOLUNTEER PANZERGRENADIER DIVISION 'NORDLAND'

A 'Germanic' Division was raised from Norwegian, Danish and Dutch volunteers in 1943, and its first operations were in November of that year, in Croatia. Within a month, 'Nordland' had been transferred to the Eastern Front. It fought there continuously, culminating in the three Battles of Courland. In March 1945, the 11th was involved in the fighting around Stettin, and from 16 April 1945, it was in action around Berlin. It then withdrew into the city, and was destroyed there.

Composition

SS Panzergrenadier Regiments No. 23 'Norge' (Norwegischer No. 1) and 24 'Danmark' (Dänischer No. 1)

Life in the front line of the Eastern Front, showing an SS trooper preparing his slit trench, with the strain of the fighting showing in his face.

16TH SS PANZERGRENADIER DIVISION 'REICHSFÜHRER SS'

This unit began life as a guard battalion for Heinrich Himmler, and in October 1943 it was enlarged on Hitler's orders to become an assault brigade. Later that year, the brigade was ordered to be expanded to divisional status, but this did not come about until June 1944. From January to April 1944, parts of one regiments of the division fought in the Anzio bridgehead, and were then pulled out of the line and posted to Hungary. Replacements for the severe loses which had been suffered came from ethnic Germans living in Hungary. After service in Italy until February 1945, the 16th was posted to Hungary, and it finished the war in eastern Austria, where it surrendered to the British Army.

Composition
SS Panzergrenadier Regiments Nos 35 and 36

17TH SS PANZERGRENADIER DIVISION 'GOETZ VON BERLICHINGEN'

Orders to raise the division were issued in October 1943, but it was not until December that this could begin, and progress remained so slow that not until May 1944 was the first divisional unit ready for action. Shortly after the Allies invaded north-west Europe, the 17th was moved to the Normandy beachhead area. For the Avranches counter-attack, the 17th was divided, with one group serving with a battle group and the other with the 2nd SS Panzer Division 'Das Reich'. During the German Army's retreat out of Normandy, 'Goetz von Berlichingen' moved eastwards via Metz, and in March the division crossed to the east bank of the Rhine. From there, it was forced to retreat through Bavaria and into the mountainous area around Bad Tölz, where it ended the war.

Composition
Panzergrenadier Regiments Nos 37 and 38

18TH SS FREIWILLIGEN PANZERGRENADIER DIVISION 'HORST WESSEL'

This formation was created during February 1944, with men recruited from the Volksdeutsche living in Hungary. It fought almost exclusively against the Jugoslav partisans.

Composition
SS Panzergrenadier Regiments Nos 39 and 40

23RD SS FREIWILLIGEN PANZERGRENADIER DIVISION 'NEDERLAND'

This unit began life as a brigade which served on the Eastern Front until it was posted to Croatia. There, the process began to upgrade it to divisional status, but this was a slow operation, and before it was completed,

The Flemish were among the most enthusiastic supporters of the German forces, and this picture shows the Flemish Legion returning from its service in Russia and parading through the streets of Antwerp.

'Nederland' was returned to the Eastern Front in January 1944. It then fought in the Courland battles. Shipped back to Stettin, the division, still not completely raised, was put into action in Pomerania before it withdrew to the Elbe, where it passed into captivity at the end of the war.

Composition
SS Freiwilligen Panzergrenadier Regiments Nos 48 'General Seyffard' (Nederländischer No. 1) and 49 'De Ruyter' (Nederländischer No. 2)

28TH FREIWILLIGEN PANZERGRENADIER DIVISION 'WALLONIEN'
This formation was raised originally as an Army unit, the 'Walloon Legion', but was taken onto the SS establishment on 1 June 1943, when it was retitled SS Freiwilligen Brigade 'Wallonien'. The brigade returned to the Eastern Front, where most of its members had already seen service, and came under command of the 5th SS Panzer Division 'Wiking'. Having suffered heavy losses, the brigade was intended to be raised anew during the spring of 1944, but before this could be completed, was posted back again to the northern sector of the Eastern Front. There, the brigade again took severe casualties. In October, the brigade was moved out of the line for rest and to be upgraded to the status of a division. The 28th had little chance to fight as a single unit, but was split up to serve with a number of individual units. At the war's end, the 28th was in Schleswig-Holstein, where its remnant was taken prisoner by the Red Army.

Composition (Winter 1944)

SS Freiwilligen Grenadier Regiments Nos 69, 70 and 71

38TH SS PANZERGRENADIER DIVISION 'NIBELUNGEN'

One of the last divisions of the Waffen-SS to be raised was Panzergrenadier Division No. 38. Hitler ordered it to be created on 27 March 1945, and further ordered that its core would be the 1,000 officer-candidates of the Junker School Bad Tölz. The SS officer-candidates, together with recently recruited soldiers of the Army and several special units, were concentrated in the Freiburg area of the Black Forest. The war's situation did not allow the formation to be completely raised, despite the arrival of reinforcements from other party units during April 1945. The incomplete division was put into action in the area of Landshut in southern Germany, where its survivors surrendered to the US Army in Reit/Winkel on 8 May.

Composition

Initially: SS Panzergrenadier Regiments Nos 1 and 2; later: SS Panzergrenadier Regiments Nos 95 and 96

PANZER GROUPS (LATER PANZER ARMIES)

PANZER GROUP 1 (LATER 1ST PANZER ARMY)

Panzer Group 1 grew out of XXII Army Corps, which was created when general mobilization was ordered in August 1939. The corps fought in Poland during the autumn of 1939, and at that time had under its command the 2nd Panzer Division and 4th Light Division. At the end of the Polish war, the corps moved to the dormant Western Front, and in the late spring of 1940, fought in the campaign in France. On 16 November 1940, the corps was upgraded and became Panzer Group 1. When Russia was invaded in June 1942, the formation fought as part of Army Group South under the command of Ewald von Kleist. Panzer Group 1 was dissolved on 5 October 1941, and immediately re-created as the 1st Panzer Army. It remained on the Eastern Front, chiefly with Army Group South, and had six different commanders: Kleist, Mackensen, Hube, Raus, Heinrici and Nehring.

PANZER GROUP 2 (LATER 2ND PANZER ARMY)

This Panzer group was created around XIX Corps on 16 November 1940, and was broken up on 5 October 1941. On that date, the group was re-created and retitled the 2nd Panzer Army. The 2nd Panzer Army served principally on the central sector of the Eastern Front, but in September 1943 was transferred to serve with Army Group F, which was operating in south-east Europe. The 2nd Panzer Army then returned to the Eastern Front, where it formed part of Army Group South from December 1944 to the end of the war in May 1945.

PANZER GROUP 3 (LATER 3RD PANZER ARMY)

Panzer Group 3 was created by upgraded XV Army Corps to Panzer Group status on 16 November 1940. On 31 December 1941, Panzer Group 3 was upgraded again and became the 3rd Panzer Army. It continued to serve on the Eastern Front, usually with Army Group Centre. Its first commander was Colonel-General Reinhardt, who was succeeded by General Raus, and finally by Colonel-General von Manteuffel.

PANZER GROUP 4 (LATER 4TH PANZER ARMY)

The 4th Panzer Army was formed out of Panzer Group 4 on 31 December 1941, and remained for the whole of its military life on the Eastern Front. It served with several major formations in the war against Russia, but mainly with Army Group South. During its time in southern Russia, the 4th fought at the approaches to Stalingrad, was later involved in the defensive battles around Stalino, and played a prominent part in the Kursk Offensive. There, it undertook what Russian historians have described as the 'Death Ride of the 4th Panzer Army'. During its military life, between 31 December 1941 and 8 May 1945, the 4th Panzer Army had eight commanders, including Hoepner, its first commanding general, and Graeser, its last.

PANZER GROUP 5 (LATER 5TH PANZER ARMY)

The unit around which the 5th Panzer Army was built was Nehring's XC Corps, which had been hastily created to defend Tunisia against the Western Allies, who had invaded that country during November 1942. The 5th, command of which passed from Nehring to von Arnim, and finally to von Vaerst, capitulated during May 1943, and was re-created on 21 August 1944 by renaming Panzer Group West, which was fighting in Normandy. The 5th served on the Western Front, notably in the fighting in the Ardennes (the Battle of the Bulge), and under the following commanders: Eberbach, Dietrich, von Manteuffel and, finally, Harpe.

PANZER GROUP 6 (LATER 6TH PANZER ARMY)

Panzer Army 6, also known as the 6th SS Panzer Army, was formed on 6 September 1944, and served on the Western Front (the Battle of the Bulge) as well as in the east (Hungary and in Austria). Its only commander was Oberstgruppenführer Sepp Dietrich.

11TH PANZER ARMY

This formation was raised on 20 January 1945, and was renamed Army Group Steiner in March 1945. As Army Group Steiner, it was given a special task by Hitler, namely to collaborate with the 9th Army and to destroy the Russian armoured spearheads which were advancing towards Berlin. Its forces were too weak to carry out the Führer's order, and after retreating westwards, it passed into Allied captivity at the end of the war.

PANZER ARMY AFRICA (AFRIKA)

The first major German formation to serve in the Italian North African colony of Libya was the German Africa Corps, which arrived in the spring of 1941. The corps was expanded to become Panzer Army Africa in January 1942, and there was a further name change in February 1943, when it became the 1st Italian Army. The first commander of the Africa Corps and then the Panzer Army Africa was Erwin Rommel, and he led it from 30 January 1942 to 9 March 1942. Illness sent him back to Germany, but he returned to take up his command on 19 March 1942, and he held it until 22 September 1942. This Panzer Army remained outside the standard numbering system for Army groups, and retained its title 'Africa' for prestige and for propaganda reasons.

Chapter Eight

Panzer Weapons

PZ KW I AUSF A

Production of this Krupp-designed tank began in July 1934, and it was the principal vehicle of the tank units. In service between 1935 and 1940, its armament was two MG 13s mounted in a turret with a 360° traverse. It was fully tracked, and weighed 5,487 kg. Its armour was 15 mm thick, and the air-cooled engine was a Krupp M305.

It was soon realized, however, that the engine design was inadequate, and modifications not only with regard to the engine, but also in its hull were made (these changes to the Ausf A resulted in the Pz Kw 1 Ausf B).

The Ausf A (and Ausf B model) were first used during the Spanish Civil War, but with the onset of the Second World War, the deficiencies in both versions were apparent, and the Pz Kw I was withdrawn almost completely by 1941.

PZ KW IV AUSF F

Rheinmetall-Borsig were responsible for development of the Pz Kw IV series, and prototypes were built during 1934–5.

The Ausf F variant appeared in 1941 after extensive modifications to the previous models, including changes in the thickness of the superstructure (its bow armour was increased to a thickness of 50 mm) as well as

A photograph of the first SP-type gun in action in the French campaign of 1940. The 4.7 cm gun with which it was armed was mounted on the chassis of a Panzer I. The crew had no protection against enemy fire, but despite that disadvantage, it remained in service until well after the opening of the war against Russia.

The Sd Kfz 232 armoured car was often used as a command vehicle, and the one shown in this photograph carries the sophisticated communications equipment required for that role.

The Ausf C variant appeared in 1937, and was the result of increased engine power and reduction gears, as well as conversions to the tracks which became standard for the Pz KW III series. It also had a rounded nose, in common with the A and B variants. The Ausf C subsequently became the basis for the production series, production beginning in December 1940.

PZ KW 38(T)

Czech vehicles were highly important to the German armed forces, and the Pz Kw 38(t), along with its variants were probably the most important of the Czech types in German service.

Production ran from 1938 until 1942, and these vehicles were very reliable and robust.

changes to the track width. There was also a resultant increase in weight.

A version of this tank later designated the Ausf F2 had a longer 7.5 cm gun fitted, the vehicle with the shorter gun being known as the Ausf F1. A special version of the Pz Kw IV, designated Pz Kw IV Ausf F – Munitions-träger für Karlgerät, was used as a munition carrier following the formation of super-heavy artillery units equipped with the Gerät 040 (Karl Mortar).

The Pz Kw IV was the backbone of the German tank arm until the end of the war.

PZ KW II AUSF C

This tank was designed as an interim model while the development of the Pz Kw III and IV types was being completed, and was based on a MAN (Maschinenfabrik Augsberg-Nürnberg) prototype. For the final development, MAN were again selected for the chassis, and Daimler-Benz for the superstructure.

An SP Panzer III and an accompanying infantry anti-tank gun crew come under fire during the advances in the early days of the war on the Russian Front.

They were equipped with a Praga EPA 7.7 litre six-cylinder petrol engine, enabling the vehicle to reach a maximum speed of 42 k.p.h. The main armament was a 3.7 cm tank gun, along with a 7.9 mm machine gun mounted in a turret.

Other variations on the 38(t) model followed. From October 1941, the 38(t) chassis was used as a reconnaissance vehicle fitted with the turret of the Sd KFz 222 armoured car.

In addition, captured Russian guns (which, ironically, were the only effective counter-weapon against the Russian T-34) were mounted on a suitably modified 38(t) chassis.

The Pz Kw 38(t) was also widely exported, and was used in the Swedish, Swiss and Peruvian Armies.

PZ KW III AUSF E

Daimler-Benz produced the first model of the Pz Kw III in 1936, and it was envisaged to

be the vehicle to equip the three light companies of tank battalions, armed with an armour-piercing weapon.

Initially, the armour was 5–14.5 mm thick, and the overall weight was 15,240 kg; the vehicle was powered by a Maybach DSO twelve-cylinder high-performance 108 TR 11 litre petrol engine, giving a top speed of 32 k.p.h. After further modifications, the Pz Kw III Ausf E variant featured the finalized chassis design of this series, and by this time weighed 19,304 kg, with 30 mm armour all round the body. The engine had also been replaced by the more powerful 120 TR, which increased maximum output to 320 h.p. (from an original 250 h.p.). The initial 3.7 cm gun was subsequently replaced by a 5 cm gun.

PANTHER V (PZ KW V)

Production of the Panther began in 1942, and the first model was the Pz Kw V Panther Ausf D. It was a heavy vehicle, ongoing

A scene from the fighting in the early days of the war with Russia. In this photograph, a Panzer III, accompanied by infantrymen, is passing through a burning village, 1941.

A variant of the Panther (Panzer V) tank, known as the Jagdpanther.

development resulting in a combat weight of 53,690 kg. A Maybach-designed 700 h.p. engine was fitted which had a capacity of 23 litres. It had a prominent gun offering good penetration, and its superstructure was steeply sloped.

An over-ambitious monthly output rate meant that vehicles were produced which quickly exhibited mechanical problems, particularly in the suspension and gears. The second production model, designated Pz Kw V Panther Ausf A, appeared in 1943, and differed from the Ausf D model in having a ball mount for the bow MG, replacing the opening hatch.

The Ausf G model appeared in 1944, and instead of its hull side plates being horizontal, as in the D and A models, they were sloped. The Ausf G was the last standard Panther to enter service in quantity.

PZ VI TIGER II

The Tiger II was the heaviest operational tank produced by any nation during the Second World War, having a weight of nearly 70,000 kg and a crew of five. It was similar in shape to the Panther, but unlike the Panther, it had very limited mobility and was unreliable. An 8.8 cm KwK 43 gun was employed, and it used the same HL 230 P 30 engine as the later production Panthers. In fact, the German Ministry of Production insisted on the Tiger II having as many common features and shared components with the planned Panther II as possible (this requirement put back completion of the Tiger II design by three months).

The Tiger II was heavily armoured, with the turret front and lower hull front having a

The Tiger (Panzer VI) variant shown in this photograph was also known as the Jagdtiger.

The 65-tonne Sturmtiger carried a 38 cm mortar whose projectile exploded with devastating effect. Only ten Sturmtigers were brought into service, and these were formed into two companies. One company fought in Warsaw, and the second in the Battle of the Bulge, December 1944.

The variant of the Tiger tank shown in this photograph was known as the Elefant, and later as the Ferdinand. It was a tank hunter, but had limited mobility.

The Brummbär was an SP weapon mounted on a Panzer IV chassis. The gun it carried was a 15 cm assault howitzer.

100 mm thickness. In hindsight, it could be argued the bulk and heavy armour of this tank reflected the defensive course the German Army was taking towards the end of the war.

STURMPANZER IV 'BRUMMBÄR'

This vehicle was effectively a Pz Kw IV tank chassis to which a relatively large and spacious superstructure had been fitted. It

The Panzer IV shown in this photograph carries armoured plate skirts to protect the tracks against hollow-charge anti-tank projectiles.

weighed just over 28,000 kg, and had a short gun in a prominent mantlet. It was designed as an infantry support vehicle for street fighting, and was in service from 1944.

JAGDPANZER V

This vehicle was the tank-destroyer version of the Panther, and was considered the best of all such vehicles. It utilized the basis chassis of the Panther, and was fitted with an enclosed turretless superstructure which held an 8.8 cm PAK gun. There was an 11° traverse, and elevation was from −8° to +14°.

Its weight was 46,738 kg, and the vehicle was heavily armoured on all sides, its front having a thickness of 80 mm. Production started in February 1944, and a total of 382 vehicles were produced, entering service before the end of the war with some Army anti-tank battalions.

It was an outstanding vehicle of its type, and possessed excellent firepower and mobility.

The Elefant, a heavy tank hunter.

SCHÜTZENPANZERWAGEN (SD KFZ 251/20)

The Sd Kfz 251/20 was fitted with a 60 cm infrared searchlight, and was intended for use in conjunction with Panther tanks also fitted with infrared sights. It was known as the Eagle Owl (Uhu).

PANZERSPÄHWAGEN (SD KFZ 234/1)

This was an eight-wheeled vehicle, and had eight-wheel drive. It had a 600 km range, and was fitted with an air-cooled diesel engine. Its weight was 10,668 kg, and enlarged balloon tyres were fitted. A maximum speed of 85 k.p.h. was possible.

The Sd Kfz 234/1 replaced the earlier eight-wheeled vehicles from 1944, and these were among the most advanced wheeled armoured vehicles to appear in the Second World War.

60 CM MORSER KARL

Also known as the Gerät 040, this was designed as a heavy bombardment weapon for siege operations. They had been initially designed to bombard the Maginot Line, but when this was overcome by other means, were used in operations on the Russian Front, notably Sebastopol and Brest-Litovsk.

The Gerät 041 was built later with a 54 cm mortar instead of the 60 cm of the Gerät 040. Six Gerät 041 vehicles were built during 1943–4.

FLAKPANZER IV

These vehicles were based on the basic Pz Kw IV chassis. The Mobelwagen was an SP AA carriage with four hinged, armoured sides; the turret was replaced by an AA mount. The Wirbelwind (2 cm gun) variant as well as the 3.7 cm Ostwind had open-topped, multi-faced, sloping turrets.

This drawing is of the Krupp's prototype for a self-propelled gun mounting an 88 mm weapon.

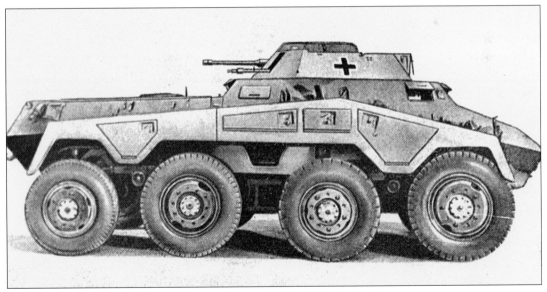

This vehicle, the first variant of the Sd Kfz 234, went into action during 1944 as part of the establishment of the armoured car battalion in Panzer divisions. The Kfz 234/1 shown in this picture carries a 2 cm gun. In later variants, the main armament was upgunned to 5 cm, and then to 7.5 cm.

From the middle years of the war, Panzer divisions needed anti-aircraft protection. This picture shows two such flak Panzers. In the foreground is the Ostwind ('East Wind'), mounting a 3.7 cm gun on a Panzer IV chassis. In the background is the Wirbelwind ('Whirlwind'), which carried four flak guns of 2 cm calibre.

The vehicle shown here is a 3.7 cm flak gun mounted on a Panzer IV chassis.

The second variant of the Sd Kfds series, the 234/2, also known as the Puma, carried a 5 cm gun in a rotating turret.

The UHU was a half-track mounting a 60 cm infrared searchlight. The UHU operated in conjunction with a Panzer tank, and would sweep the area for targets. Details of any which were located were passed back to the Panzer, which was also fitted with an infrared light.

Flakpanzer IVs were used in service with anti-aircraft platoons in tank regiments from 1944; 150 Wirbelwind were in service with anti-aircraft platoons of tank battalions from 1944, and 40 Ostwind served with anti-aircraft platoons of tank regiments from 1945.

The Wirbelwind and Ostwind designs could also fire their weapons against ground targets.

FLAKPANZER 'KUGELBLITZ'

This A/A vehicle featured a hemispherical turret with twin aircraft-type cannon. As with the other Flakpanzer variants, the chassis and basic superstructure were of the Pz Kw IV design. Only six of these expensive vehicles ever reached service towards the end of the war, but they were very serviceable.

'MAULTIER' PANZERWERFER

This vehicle utilized a Nebelwerfer gun which had 2 × 5 rocket tubes, and had a flat, sloping rear. It entered service from 1944 with Panzerwerfer battalions.

WEAPONS CARRIERS

The Waffenträger Große 1 'large weapons carrier' was designed towards the end of 1944, and incorporated the 10.5 cm leFJ 18/40 L/28 light field howitzer. The gun could be removed from the chassis and placed on its normal field mount. Its combat weight was 14,224 kg.

The Waffenträger Große II was developed in 1944 to accommodate the 12.8 cm L/55 gun. Its combat weight was 18,065 kg, and the vehicle had a very low profile.

CHAPTER NINE

THE ARTILLERY

According to Reibert's *Handbook of the German Army,* 'through its fire, the artillery supports the infantry, both in attack as well as in defence, by engaging targets which are behind cover'. That definition confirmed the artillery's role as a supporting arm. For that task, it was equipped with weapons whose fire could engage any target met on the battlefield. Thus the artillery arm included not only the standard types of gun and howitzer, but also assault guns, fortress and coastal batteries, heavy and super-heavy weapons, the Army's anti-aircraft (Flak) detachments, smoke troops, anti-gas units and the cartography department.

Since the artillery supported the infantry – the principal arm of service – it, like the other support services, was formed into a pool of formations from which the OKW took units as they were needed. The artillery, like the other arms, was not organized by divisions, but by regiments. The intention to link a numbered artillery regiment to a similarly numbered infantry division was seldom realized, and with the Army's expansion, the serial system broke down. Only in the third and fourth waves could the differences in numbering be temporarily, and then only partially, resolved.

A PAK 40 anti-tank gun in action on the Eastern Front.

The artillery was arranged regimentally because it was not foreseen that a larger grouping than a regiment would be needed. That optimistic belief was soon shown to be false. In October 1943, a crisis on a sector held by Army Group Centre led to the decision to amalgamate a number of regiments into the 18th Artillery Division, a formation which was not broken up until April 1944. The successful deployment of the 18th Division led to the creation by Army Group South of Artillery Divisions 310–312 and, in north-west Europe, to the creation of Artillery Division 309. At the same time as moves were being made to group artillery regiments into divisions, other moves were afoot to form Army artillery brigades, of which Nos 401–410 were created. Those brigades had only a short life, and were soon converted to become Volksartillerie Korps. This description was a misnomer, for these were not corps in the accepted sense of that term, but just artillery regiments with a greater than usual number of battalions.

The planned organization of artillery regiments attached to infantry divisions had foreseen a regimental HQ and an HQ battery (the latter only after 1942), together with three light battalions each of three batteries of 10.5 cm howitzers. Each battery fielded four guns. In addition, there was a heavy battalion with an HQ battery and three batteries of 15 cm howitzers. Thus it was intended that each regiment would have an arsenal of forty-eight guns, and that these would be horse-drawn. An example of the shortages of home-produced weapons which began to show themselves as early as the middle years of the war was the fact that some divisions of later waves had to be equipped with Czech guns, while others were outfitted with French weapons.

As new infantry divisions were raised, the artillery weapons to outfit them were taken from existing regiments and handed over to the newly raised formations. Soon it became apparent that the war establishment of artillery regiments in infantry divisions was no longer being met, and a thorough reorganization was carried through in the main divisional types. In the standard infantry formation, the light battalions had two batteries each of four 10.5 cm howitzers and a light field gun battery of six 7.5 cm pieces as well as a heavy howitzer battalion equipped with six 15 cm pieces. The war establishment of Gebirgs artillery regiments and the artillery regiments of Panzer divisions also underwent changes, and the composition of artillery regiments in the 'Panzer Division 1943 Pattern', and the subsequent '1944 Pattern' illustrates this.

The heavy artillery of the German Army also consisted of independent regiments. The initial establishment of 35 battalions which existed at the outbreak of war rose to 117 by May 1940. The heaviest artillery pieces were represented by those weapons with calibres above 21 cm – those of 24, 30.5 or 42 cm. The barrels for many of these pieces were taken from naval vessels which were no longer in commission. By contrast, the super-heavy pieces (those of 60 cm and 80 cm calibre) had been designed before the war, and were introduced immediately after hostilities began. They had been constructed to be used against the fortifications of the Maginot Line, but were not deployed during that campaign in the west, but were used, with limited success, on the Eastern Front, against forts in the Crimea and against targets in Leningrad.

At the most senior level of the artillery command structure, there were generals of artillery serving on the staff of each Army group. The OKW intention to appoint an artillery commander to every infantry division was not realized, and it was not until late in the war that each corps had one such officer on its staff.

CHAPTER TEN

ARTILLERY WEAPONS

INFANTRY ARTILLERY

The Germans introduced four main artillery pieces prior to and during the Second World War, and apart from the 15 cm Schweres Infanteriegeschütz 33 issued in 1927, were restricted to a 7.5 cm calibre. Lightness and ease of use were priorities.

Rheinmetall-Borsig AG (formerly Rheinische Metallwaren- und Maschinenfabrik, or RM&M) were the principal manufacturers of these guns, specializing in weapons having a calibre of 17 cm and below.

The four principal guns were as follows.

Although designed as a light anti-aircraft gun, the 2 cm Flak was found to be useful in engaging ground targets. When all four barrels of the Flak Vierling were employed the effect was devastating. This photograph, taken during the final stages of the war in Jugoslavia, shows a Flak Vierling operating against targets on the ground.

A horse-drawn heavy gun changing its firing position and moving through the sandy soil of eastern Poland during the first advances into Russia, 1941.

7.5 CM LEICHTES INFANTERIEGESCHÜTZ 18 (7.5 CM LE IG 18 (FERELLE))

This was developed by Rheinmetall, one of the two principal manufacturers, and was used during the years between 1927 and 1945. It employed an unusual shotgun-breech action and a simple box trail as a carriage. A lighter version was introduced in 1937 for use by mountain troops. In addition, a virtually identical model for use by airborne and parachute forces was also tested, but not introduced.

Weight in action	400 kg
Length of gun	88.4 cm
Length of bore	78.3 cm
Elevation	−10° to +75°
Traverse	12°
Ammunition	Several variations on the standard high-explosive shell, e.g. 7.5 cm I Gr 18: Fused AZ 23, 6.00 kg
Propelling charge	Five-part charge consisting of five bundles of perforated discs of propellant, each held together with thread and labelled with the portion number
Primer	Standard C/12nA percussion primer

7.5 CM INFANTERIEGESCHÜTZ 37 (7.5 CM IG37)

This was introduced in 1944, using carriages recaptured from the Russians (after initially selling them with the 3.7 cm gun), and utilizing a coil-spring suspension. This new, Krupp-

This artillery piece, dragged into position on the summit of the Asu mountain, dominated the Red Army's positions in the upper Baksam valley, some 3,500 m below. The Caucasus, 1942.

On the Eastern Front, rank was of little importance when it came to moving a vehicle which was stuck in Russian mud. Here, field officers are helping to push out an infantry gun.

designed gun had an unusual vertical sliding-block breech and a four-baffle muzzle brake.

7.5 CM INFANTERIEGESCHÜTZ 42 (7.5 CM IG 42 (GRAUWOLF))

Initially dropped by the infantry, this weapon was reintroduced when it was clear that something new was needed. The gun used came from the early IG37 (indeed, the carriage was the only difference between the two weapons), and an angled shield was fitted.

15 CM SCHWERE INFANTERIEGESCHÜTZ 33 (15 CM S IG33)

The 15 cm calibre was the largest ever issued as an infantry gun. Few were made, however, due to the light alloys required for production being monopolized by the Luftwaffe.

MOUNTAIN ARTILLERY

Mountain campaigns imposed their own special demands on the nature of weapons used. As well as needing to be light and easy to assemble and break down, other factors such as increased carriage flexibility (necessary for effective firing up- and downhill) needed to be incorporated into the design specification.

7.5 CM GEBIRGSKANONE 15 (7.5 CM GEB K15)

This weapon was distinguished by the presence of a heavy jacket surrounding the barrel, known as a 'slipper', which aided removal and improved stability, due to the extra weight. The carriage had wooden-spoked wheels and a shield.

A mountain artillery battalion bringing its weapons forward on the backs of mules. The mountain guns could be broken down into loads, and these would be carried by animals or, when the terrain was too difficult, on the backs of the Jäger. Jugoslavia, 1943.

7.5 CM GEBIRGSGESCHÜTZ 36 (7.5 CM GEB G36 (GRUNEWALD))

This entered service in 1938, and was used throughout the war. It had no shield, and due to its lightness was relatively unstable, liable to jump when fired at low elevation.

Weight in action	58.2 kg
Length of gun	1.63 cm
Length of bore	97.3 cm
Elevation	$-5°$ to $+70°$
Traverse	$40°$
Ammunition	Separate-loading, cased charge
Performance	Firing high-explosive shell

7.5 CM GEBIRGSGESCHÜTZ 43 (7.5 CM GEB G43 (HALNSEE))

Although designed to be more stable than its predecessor, the G36, development of the G43 was halted due to other priorities.

10.5 CM GEBIRGSHAUBITZE 40 (10.5 CM GEB H40 (EBERESCHE))

Appearing in 1942, this Bohler-designed weapon was the heaviest mountain weapon ever developed, and so good was its performance that some pieces were still in use well into the 1960s. Despite its top-heavy appearance, its triangular base gave good support in all terrain.

FIELD ARTILLERY

Weaponry ranged from 7.5 cm to 10.5 cm guns and howitzers, although the smaller calibre was finding favour again through the 1940s; it was felt that the trade-off between losing shellpower and gaining flexibility and adaptability was well worth the transition back to 7.5 cm weapons, and this could be largely overcome anyway by using updated versions of ammunition used in the old 7.7 cm weapons. In addition, the German

A far cry from the years of mobility and victory. Even at the outbreak of the war, a great number of German artillery weapons were horse-drawn, and by the end of the war, oxen and other cattle had to be employed in the more primitive areas of south-eastern Europe, as this picture shows.

Army adopted the so-called 'golf-bag system' of carrying a variety of weapons onto the battlefield to cover any eventuality in action, so a range of calibres was maintained. The supply of weapons was further augmented by using guns captured in action, particularly those from the Polish and the French.

7.5 CM FELDKANONE 7M85 (7.5 CM FK 7M85 (WANNSEE))

This weapon was introduced as a light, dual-purpose field/anti-tank gun. However, due to the hashing together of the component parts (derived from the gun, cradle and recoil system of the 10 cm le FH 18/40 and the carriage of the 7.5 cm PAK 40), it turned out to be overweight, but it did have greater elevation (an additional 50°) and a greater range of ammunition.

10.5 CM LEICHTE FELDHAUBITZE 18 (10.5 CM LE FH 18 (OPLADEN))

This weapon was developed by Rheinmetall, and replaced the obsolete le FH 16. It became the standard field howitzer, and had a good reputation for stability and reliability. The recoil system followed the pattern of the 7.5 cm FK 18, where the hydro-pneumatic recuperator was above the barrel, with the buffer contained in the cradle. After the war, it could still be found in the Albanian, Bulgarian and Hungarian Armies.

10.5 CM LEICHTE FELDHAUBITZE 42 (10.5 CM LE FH42)

Despite the fact that this weapon was to replace the 18, 18M and 18/40 howitzers, its specification was obsolete by the time the design was completed, and the le FH 42 was not accepted for service. The Russian campaign had illustrated the need to be able to fire at high angles of elevation (above 45°), due to forested regions where fighting was taking place, and a revised specification which became the le FH 43 was issued.

The weapons of the German Field Artillery included several which had been introduced as anti-aircraft guns but which were found to be particularly effective as anti-tank guns. This picture shows an 88 mm gun being towed into action behind a half-track vehicle.

Weight in action	1,630 kg
Length of gun	294 cm
Length of bore	Not known
Elevation	$-5°-+45°$
Traverse	70°
Ammunition	As for the le FH 18M and 18/40, but note that the firing system of the le FH 42 was electric
Performance	Firing standard shell weighing 14.8 kg

HEAVY FIELD ARTILLERY

15 CM SCHWERE FELDHAUBITZE 36 (15 CM FH 36)

This was a Rheinmetall-Borsig design, and was developed to provide a lighter version of the s FH 18. A shorter barrel than the s FH 18 and an alloy-based carriage helped achieve this. The gun could be disconnected and drawn back onto the cradle extension for travelling, and the quick-release system was interlocked to the breechlock; this prevented the block opening or the firing pin being released if the gun was not securely locked to the recoil system. The carriage was a split-trail type with alloy wheels. As light-weight alloys were in short supply, production stopped in 1942.

Weight in action	3,280 kg
Length of gun	380.5 cm
Length of bore	247.4 cm
Elevation	0–45°
Traverse	56°
Ammunition	Separate-loading, cased charge
Performance	Standard high-explosive shell, 43.5 kg

15 CM SCHWERE FELDHAUBITZE 18/43 (15 CM S FH 18/43)

A shortage of cartridge-case metal and production capability led designers to look anew at a bag-charge loading system, and this weapon represented a departure from the traditional cartridge-loading system. Manufacture of the type of breech used in a bag-charge loading system involved specialized machinery, as well as specialized and perfected firing mechanisms and a resilient pad. Germany had always employed the sliding-block breech and metallic cartridge case in all calibres, and had never shown much interest in the bag-charge system, but the metal shortage changed this. Despite this fresh approach, like the FH 36, the FH 18/42 never entered service.

15 CM KANONE 39 (15 CM K 39)

This weapon was to be used as a coast defence gun, as well as in its usual field role. Initially manufactured to a design requested by the Turkish Army, most of the consignment was taken over by the Germans when war commenced. When used as a coastal weapon, the turntable platform along with its steel assembly was fixed firmly to the ground using anchors. Traverse was achieved using a hand crank.

RAILWAY ARTILLERY

28 CM KANONE 5 IN EISENBAHNLAFETTE (28 CM K 5 (E))

The K 5 became the standard Army railway gun. Design began in 1934, and weapons entered service in 1936. Designed as a super-long-range weapon using deep-grooved barrels and splined projectiles, four types entered service. The K 5 Tiefzug 10 mm was the first, the barrel made with twelve 10 mm grooves. However, after a series of split barrels, the depth of the grooves was reduced to 7 mm – the result was the K 5 Tiefzug 7 mm. The K 5 Vz was also developed, and had a multi-grooved barrel. Finally, a version

In the German Army, heavy and super-heavy guns were considered to be particularly effective. For ease of mobility, they were often mounted on railway trucks in the fashion of this 28 cm piece.

with a bored-out barrel was produced, designed to fire Peenemunde arrow shells. As well as the four versions of the K 5, thought was also given to extending the range, and to this end a rocket-assisted shell was issued, the propellant in the nose section ignited by a time fuse after 19 seconds in flight. In 1943, the Army expressed interest in a weapon which was capable of being deployed even when the rail track had been destroyed, and which would also be capable of being transported on the chassis and running gear of the Tiger tank. However, the project was still in the development stage when the war ended.

Weight in action	218,000 kg
Length of gun	2,154 cm
Length of bore	2,055 cm
Elevation	0–50°
Traverse	1° on the carriage
Ammunition	Separate-loading, cased charge
Performance	Standard pre-rifled shell, 255.5 kg

Many of the heavy artillery pieces used during the Second World War had been introduced during the First World War, and this mortar was one such piece.

80 CM KANONE IN EISENBAHNLAFETTE 'GUSTAV GERÄT' (80 CM K (E))

Eventually the largest gun ever made, this outlandish weapon was not initially considered a serious project, but this changed after Hitler's visit to the Krupp factory in 1936. Calculations performed after the Army Weapons Office had enquired about the viability of 70, 80 or 100 cm calibre guns were given to Hitler when he made the same enquiries at the factory; in addition, Gustav Krupp von Bohlen and Halbach shrewdly initiated design work on the 80 cm model. In 1937, the design was approved, and manufacture began that summer. There were, unsurprisingly, teething problems with assembling such a huge weapon, and the original deadline of spring 1940 was missed – it was eventually completed early in 1942. By this time, a second weapon was also ready for despatch (codenamed 'Dora', after the designer's wife), and a third was being constructed. 'Gustav' was employed to spectacular effect at the siege of Sebastopol, but practice as well as service shots had worn out the barrel, and it was sent to Essen to be re-lined. Transport and assembly was a massive undertaking, employing nearly 1,500 men and taking up to three weeks to prepare the site and erect the gun – resources that might, with hindsight, have been used to better effect elsewhere.

CHAPTER ELEVEN

THE OTHER ARMS OF SERVICE

In addition to the arms of service which the German Army considered to be the fighting echelons – infantry, artillery and armour – there were others which supported the combat arms, including engineers, signals, medical and veterinary units, the transportation corps and the military police.

Under the 'unity of command' principle, those units which were considered non-combatant were used as a pool from which the high command could draw the units it considered necessary to carry out a military task or operation. Consequently, although such units were attached to an Army or an Army Group, this was not a permanent assignment, and they could be deployed to serve with any formation of that or another Army or Army Group.

The hierarchical structure of such units was therefore not divisional, but regimental, or more usually by battalion.

THE CAVALRY

Even before the outbreak of the Second World War, the cavalry had lost its status as one of the main arms of service, and its strength was reduced to that of a single brigade. This demotion may have been due to Hitler's dislike of horses, or else his intention to have a fully mechanized Army in which cavalry would have no role.

If his was the latter intention, then that was never realized. The German Army never achieved full mechanization, and throughout the war, 80 per cent of the Army's motive power depended upon horses, used chiefly to tow the artillery pieces. When Operation BARBAROSSA, the invasion of the Soviet Union, opened in June 1941, more than 750,000 beasts took part, and during the war on the Eastern Front, more than 2½ million horses served. The losses they suffered were enormous, and it has been calculated that an average of 1,000 beasts died or were killed each day of that conflict. It has further been calculated that 17 per cent of all horse casualties were due to heart failure brought about by the strain of towing the guns through the mud of the Eastern Front. Such a high rate of loss required vast remount operations to recoup, and these were carried out, not in Russia alone, but throughout the whole of Continental Europe.

The course of operations on the Eastern Front soon showed how short-sighted had been the German Army's abolition of horsed formations and how short-sighted it continued to be despite evidence that cavalry patrols were more efficient than any other type. As early as 3 November 1941, the cavalry arm, which had risen from brigade strength to become a division, was abolished, and converted to become the 24th Panzer Division. There was no longer a cavalry presence in the German Army, but the experience of the troops in the field proved that a demand existed for patrols which could move faster than infantry or could cross terrain impassable to armour. Mounted units were organized unofficially by divisions fighting in crisis areas, and by the summer of 1943, two regiments had been created and fielded. Although, officially, the German Army no longer had a cavalry division, one had been raised from the Cossack peoples of the Soviet Union. This formation, which was created in August 1943, comprised two brigades supported by a Caucasian artillery battalion. Later a 2nd and then a 3rd Cossack Division were formed, and these were combined into a corps. Late in 1944, that corps was transferred *en bloc* from the Army into the SS, an organization which still maintained horsed units on its establishment. The SS cavalry units were formed into the SS Cavalry Division 'Florian Geyer' shortly after the outbreak of war, and later, during the war, two other SS cavalry divisions were formed.

THE 8TH SS CAVALRY DIVISION 'FLORIAN GEYER'

Heinrich Himmler's order of May 1940 was for the creation of a 1st and 2nd Cavalry Standarte. In August of the following year, these were amalgamated to form a cavalry brigade, and were put into action on the Eastern Front to clear partisan-infested rear areas. That two-regiment formation was raised to a division during June 1942 and, in November 1944, had the name 'Florian Geyer' added to its title.

The divisional order of battle in 1942 was two mounted regiments supported by an artillery battalion, and that establishment increased during the summer of 1943, when a third mounted regiment was raised. In the autumn of that year, there was a change in regimental description and numbering when

they became cavalry regiments Nos 15, 16, 17 and 18.

The 'Florian Geyer' Cavalry Division spent the greatest part of its time on the Eastern Front on anti-partisan operations, during which time it was switched from one sector to another. While serving as part of the garrison of Budapest, it was destroyed in the fighting, and the intention to re-raise it was not realized.

22ND SS FREIWILLIGEN CAVALRY DIVISION

In April 1944, Heinrich Himmler ordered the raising of a Freiwilligen Cavalry Division around a cadre of the 17th Regiment of the 'Florian Geyer' Division. The component parts of the newly created 22nd Division saw action even before it had been completely raised, and they fought in Debreczen and then in Budapest, where the major part of the division was taken prisoner. The intention to re-raise the 22nd was never realized.

In September 1944, its order of battle was: SS Freiwilligen Cavalry Regiment No. 1, which was renumbered No. 52 from October, Regiment No. 2, which was renumbered as No. 53, and Regiment No. 3, which from October became Regiment No. 17.

37TH SS FREIWILLIGEN CAVALRY DIVISION 'LUETZOW'

During February 1945, Himmler ordered that a division was to be created out of the two SS cavalry divisions which had been destroyed in Budapest. The newly created formation was put into action in April 1945, and positioned between the German 6th and 8th Armies to the north of Vienna. The division received the name 'Luetzow' during this time. It was forced to retreat through Austria, and reached the American lines, where it surrendered.

The order of battle was SS Cavalry Regiments Nos 92 and 93.

THE COSSACK CAVALRY CORPS

This was created during November 1944, when Himmler ordered the amalgamation of the Cossack Division with other Army Cossack formations, those of the Waffen-SS and of the police.

The new formation was numbered 14th SS Corps.

THE MEDICAL SERVICE

The German Army laid great emphasis on maintaining the health of its soldiers. In addition to prophylactic measures such as unit hygiene, dentistry, inoculations and eye care, the evacuation and treatment of the wounded was its first priority.

The organization of the medical corps was by battalion (Armee Sanitätsabteilung), one of which was allocated to an Army in the field. That battalion controlled the field hospitals, usually four in number. Its subordinate formations were companies, each of which controlled one field hospital and an ambulance detachment.

A soldier wounded on the battlefield would be picked up by stretcher-bearers of his own unit, and if they were unable to treat his wounds, he would be evacuated to a casualty clearing station. Arriving at that place, a soldier with non-serious wounds would be treated until he was fit enough to return to his unit. More serious cases would be dealt with at an Army field hospital (Armee Feldlazarett). Soldiers with wounds which required major surgery would be passed along the medical evacuation route until they were admitted into a general hospital (Kriegslazarett). When his wounds were healed, the soldier would pass into convalescence and then back to the regimental depot, from which he would be returned to his own unit. The nature of the wounds which the Kriegslazarett treated required that the buildings were sited in stable, well-lit and quiet premises, and most general hospitals were set up in large towns with access to running water and an adequate sewage disposal system.

A medical company in the field, which, as stated above, controlled a field hospital, was sub-divided into platoons which worked in the casualty clearing stations. There was a very efficient evacuation and/or treatment system, and because the German Army was run on internal lines of operation, it was possible for a wounded man to be evacuated along the line and to be given a berth in a hospital train which would carry him to a hospital back in the Reich.

Among the other units administered by the medical branch were anti-gas decontamination companies, as well as platoons which dealt with disinfestation of buildings or soldiers.

The prophylactic measures referred to earlier also covered the civil population in the war zone, particularly those in eastern and south-eastern Europe, where medical facilities were either poor or non-existent. Doctors of the German Army's medical service, and also those of the SS, were active in treating civilians and in carrying out such measures as spraying stagnant water to prevent malaria.

ENGINEERS

The engineer branch of the German Army included units which not only carried out the tasks of mine-laying and lifting, bridge-building, tunnelling and road construction, repairing railway tracks and carrying out demolitions, but also included teams which carried out the duties of assault infantry. Those groups of assault engineers spearheaded attacks, blew up barbed-wire entanglements using 'Bangalore torpedoes', smashed enemy opposition in blockhouses

Assault engineers crossing the River Meuse during the 1940 campaign in the west. The craft being used is a standard man-powered inflatable boat.

Troops undergoing river crossing training on an inflated assault craft.

The pioneer units of the Army were equipped with motorized assault boats. These were especially useful on the Eastern Front, where they were needed to cross the wide rivers of the Soviet Union.

The rapid transmission of orders and the fast action taken in response to them were the keys to the successes enjoyed by the Panzer arm of service. In this photograph, Guderian is seen in his command vehicle with the communications systems which he used to pass orders. In the foreground is the Enigma machine.

or bunkers through the use of demolition charges, and operated flame-throwers.

Organization was by regiment, which broke down to battalions, and then to individual companies.

SIGNALS

The military author, Franz Kurowski, stated in one of his works that every fifth soldier in the German Army of the Second World War was in the signals arm of service. Great importance was laid upon intercepting enemy wireless messages, and on swiftly transmitting their content so that prompt action could be taken. There is no doubt that the German wireless intercept service was

highly efficient, and during the war in North Africa, the British 8th Army launched a special operation to destroy Captain Seebohm's detachment, which was considered to be one of the most efficient in the German Army.

The German Army's signals branch's organization went no higher than regiment level, with the lowest level being that of a field company. It was usual for a signals battalion – the intermediate level – to be allotted to a division, and for a regiment to form part of an Army's or an Army Group's establishment.

In common with the other arms of service, the numbering system of signals units ran from 1 to 999, although not all

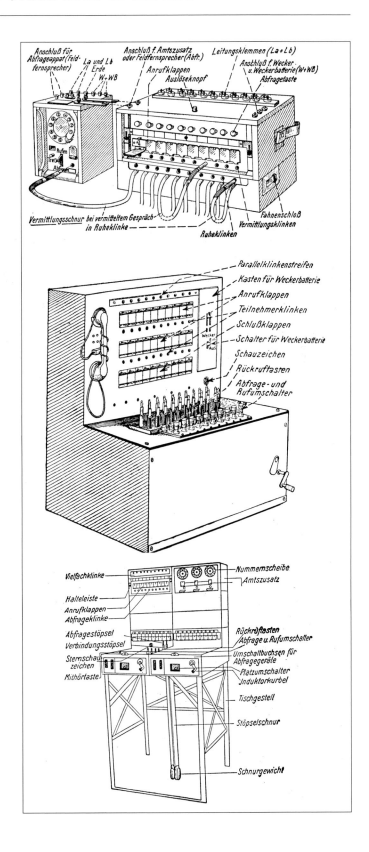

A ten-line telephone exchange.

An advanced outpost of the 'Großdeutschland' Division, showing the field telephone exchange (the ten-line exchange).

In May 1944, an attempt was made to destroy Tito and his headquarters through an airborne assault. This picture shows the signals centre of the SS para unit which carried out the assault.

A senior officer of signals testing equipment at the Army Group HQ communications terminal.

carried on horse-drawn carts, the ubiquitous Panjewagen.

The equipment issued to signals units was well-designed and robust in construction, with sets which ranged across a wide spectrum, from field telephone sets, to ten-line subscriber networks and teleprinters, as well as transmitters and receivers of several strengths.

MILITARY POLICE

There were three basic types of police force: the Military Police (Feldgendarmerie), the Secret Field Police (Geheime Feldpolizei) and the Traffic Police (Vekehrsregelung-polizei). Units of all three were allocated by battalion to an Army or a Panzer Army. The basic organization broke down into troops or groups which were distributed as needed in the Army's rear areas or in the zones of occupation.

Feldgendarmerie units wore uniform details that distinguished them from the other types: a cloth badge worn on the upper left arm, showing an oak wreath within which was an eagle and a swastika. They also carried a cuff title with the word 'Feldgendarmerie' in silver thread.

The second military police type, the Secret Field Police, were organized in groups, the size and strength of which depended upon local conditions. A group was usually in company strength when it was seconded to an Army or Army Group, but was of battalion size when it formed part of the Army of Occupation.

The third type of military police formation specialized in traffic control. On the Eastern Front, the number of roads was fewer than in western Europe, and they were not capable of carrying heavy traffic. On military operations in which masses of men, AFVs and carts were on the move, it was essential that movement schedules be

the numbers were taken up, so there were gaps in the sequence. Attempts to ally a Signals formation to a similarly numbered major unit (i.e. No. 1 Signals Battalion to the 1st Infantry Division, and the 1st Motorized Signals Regiment to the 1st Panzer Army) did not work in practice. Signals units attached to a mountain division bore the distinguishing title 'Gebirgs', and battalions on the strength of Panzer and Panzergrenadier divisions carried the description 'Motorized', and were an integral part of those mobile formations. Signals battalions attached to infantry divisions were equipped only with transport to carry the wireless equipment. The signallers either marched or were

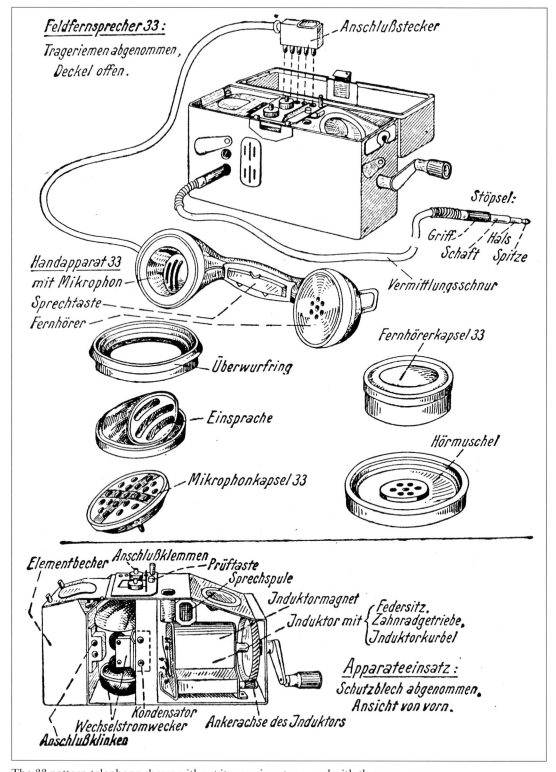

Feldfernsprecher 33:
Trageriemen abgenommen,
Deckel offen.

Anschlußstecker

Stöpsel:
Griff   Hals
Schaft   Spitze

Vermittlungsschnur

Handapparat 33
mit Mikrophon
Sprechtaste
Fernhörer

Überwurfring

Fernhörerkapsel 33

Einsprache

Hörmuschel

Mikrophonkapsel 33

Elementbecher   Anschlußklemmen   Prüftaste
Sprechspule

Jnduktormagnet

Jnduktor mit { Federsitz.
Zahnradgetriebe.
Jnduktorkurbel

Apparateeinsatz:
Schutzblech abgenommen.
Ansicht von vorn.

Kondensator
Wechselstromwecker   Ankerachse des Jnduktors
Anschlußklinken

The 33 pattern telephone shown without its carrying straps and with the cover open.

enforced and allotted roads strictly controlled. The battalions of Traffic Police carried out those functions, and their units were deployed as required, either by battalion or by company.

THE VETERINARY SERVICE

The veterinary service was concerned chiefly with the treatment of horses and mules which had fallen sick or which had been wounded on active service. The organization of this service was usually by company, and it was a unit of that size which administered the Army horse hospitals (Armee Pferde-lazaretten), as well as organizing the motorized horse transport column.

THE TRANSPORT ARM AND ITS VEHICLES

The German Army's transport service was not supplied either with abundant or first-class equipment, for it included many civilian vehicles which had been adapted to military use. Given that poor state of production and issue, it is surprising that the transportation service functioned as well as it did. The output of trucks from German factories and the scale of issue of those vehicles could never match the numbers of first-class lorries which were supplied to the Allied armies. There was no Reich plan for a national mass production of wheeled military vehicles, so the most usual method of meeting the Army's requirements was through requisitioning or confiscation. Thus a

In the German services, the Volkswagen car was the equivalent of the Jeep in the Allied armies. The one shown is on active service in North Africa.

One version of the Volkswagen was the amphibious version, known as the Schwimmwagen. On the second vehicle of this column can be seen the Schwimmwagen propellor inside its protective ring.

German transport column on active service might contain, in addition to standard military lorries, those of civilian pattern, motor coaches and even private cars. The demand for spare parts for this miscellany of vehicles must have been almost impossible to resolve. Wear and tear on civilian vehicles which had been built to run on smooth roads and which, on active service, were forced to plough their way through Russian mud must have led to innumerable breakdowns.

The organization of the transport arm of service was usually by battalion, although more than fifty military transport regiments were raised, chiefly to carry troops. In addition to the regiments, there were also military transport battalions and independent companies to carry out vehicle and tank repair, recovery and maintenance. At a higher level than the regiment, there were Army and high command transport parks, whose establishments included the units listed above. In addition to regiments, battalions and companies, there were independent platoons for the supply of petrol and water.

The principal vehicles of the transportation branch, included those made by Daimler-Benz, Buessing, Hansa-Lloyd (Borgward), Demag, Hanomag and Famo. Most of the trucks were petrol-driven, and one of the requirements when issuing contracts was that a lorry built for one purpose could be speedily converted to carry out other tasks. It was only later in the war that specialized transport types were built, and these were usually prime movers or tank transporters.

The most common medium or heavy lorry types included the Opel Blitz, 31.6t-36 S, a 3 tonne lorry to which specialized bodies could be fitted over the basic chassis. There were three types of Opel, of which the 3.6t-36 S was the military version. This had two-wheel drive, and the two rear wheels provided the motive power. The water-cooled engine was petrol-driven, and could develop 68 b.h.p. Four forward gears were fitted, and one reverse gear.

The type 6700 A Opel truck was a four-wheel-drive version of the 3.6. It also had a set of transfer gears, one of which was used for road travel, and the second for cross-country driving.

The German-built versions of the 3 ton Ford, the G 917 T and the G 997 T, were both civilian vehicles modified to meet military requirements. Both were two-wheel-drive trucks and were powered by V8 water-cooled engines which developed 78 b.h.p.

The Mercedes-Benz vehicles which were supplied to the German Army included a 3 tonne lorry, type LCF 3000, which had a strongly built chassis. The vehicle was diesel-powered, with a four-cylinder water-cooled engine. There were the usual four forward speeds and one reverse. The LCF 3000 was a two-wheel-drive vehicle.

Other lorries of the Mercedes series were in the 10 tonne class, and the Buessing NAG 4.5 tonne truck was another of the standard trucks with which the Army was supplied.

LIGHT VEHICLES

The standard light car was a military version of the Volkswagen, whose touring body had a folding top. The air-cooled four-cylinder engine was mounted at the rear of the vehicle, and could develop 24.5 b.h.p. There were four forward speeds and one reverse. The Volkswagen, which was a two-wheel-drive machine, could attain a speed of 80 k.p.h.

There was an amphibious version of the Volkswagen, known as the Schwimmwagen ('swim-car'). The crankshaft was extended to the rear of the body, where it engaged the propeller shaft by means of a dog-clutch. When the Schwimmwagen was travelling across country, the propeller and shaft folded over the back of the vehicle.

Among the other types of car were the Hanomag Type 325, the Stoewer Type R 180 W and AW 2, and the Mercedes-Benz Type 170 V.

These medium and heavy cars were more sturdily built than the Volkswagen, and the heavy car could be used for a variety of purposes, including as a prime mover for light artillery.

CHAPTER TWELVE

FLAGS AND COLOURS

From the earliest days of recorded history, groups of men going out to war have taken with them an emblem which symbolized their tribal, racial or national allegiance, and which was thus the focus of their common will. As early as medieval times, that emblem had become a flag, and on the field of battle, it inspired the soldiers when it was carried before them in an attack, or it served as a rallying point during a retreat or in some other desperate situation. Over the centuries, the unit flag – the regimental colour – became so revered an object that to lose it in battle was the bitterest disgrace which could befall a regiment.

Units of the German Army still carried colours with them into action at the start of the First World War, and when the practice was discontinued in the final years of that conflict, these were laid up in museums, local government buildings or in churches. Following the end of the First World War, there was a period of more than twenty years during which no unit colours were presented, for this was the period of the Weimar Republic, a strongly anti-military, socialist regime. The negative attitude of the Weimar government was reversed during the early years of the Nazi government, when on 16 March 1936, an

Two photographs showing the Reichskriegflagge being hoisted in Athens at the conclusion of the campaign in Greece, 1941.

One of the earliest parades during which colours were presented to Army units. The photograph shows guidons and standards being presented by General von Reichenau. Note the carrying sashes, the piped parade tunic, the Marksmanship lanyard on the right shoulder of the nearest man, and the gorgets around the neck worn by the NCOs carrying the colours.

official announcement stated that new standards were to be presented to units of the Luftwaffe on 21 April 1936. Colours were presented to the other arms of service chiefly in 1936–7.

Not just on a military level, but also at a national level there had been another break with the Weimar government's attitudes. Under that regime, the national flag had been a tricolour in black, red and gold and,

shortly after the Nazis came to power in January 1933, an order was issued which restored the national colours to a tricolour in the traditional red, white and black. On official occasions, flags of that type were flown, together with the Nazi Party's swastika banner. There was also another official flag: the national war banner (Reichskriegsflagge). This was a red field upon which was placed a cross in bands of alternate white and black, and in the centre of that cross, a swastika set in a black-and-white circle. In a canton in the top left-hand corner was the emblem of the Iron Cross.

There were also command flags designed for use by Hitler and the leaders of the three fighting services. Miniatures of those flags carried on one of the wings of the official car were held inside a clear, plastic cover to protect them against the elements.

As mentioned above, Luftwaffe units received the first unit colours of the Nazi era, and nearly five months were to pass before the first Army units received theirs. There were sixteen units on parade on 14 September 1936, when regimental standards were bestowed upon a group which included infantry, motorized infantry, Panzer, cavalry, reconnaissance, signals and artillery formations. That first parade was followed by a succession of others, including one when regiments of what had been the Austrian Army handed over their formal standards and received new ones. The final presentation of colours was held in Danzig, where units of the Replacement Army (Ersatzheer) received theirs in 1940.

The standard-sized regimental flag was a 125 cm square piece of silk in arm-of-service colour: white for infantry, green for Jäger, and red for artillery, etc. On the obverse, and occupying most of the field, was an Iron Cross. The centre of the flag was a white disc surrounded by a wreath of silver oakleaves, within which was a Wehrmacht eagle

The new army. Infantry units with their newly presented regimental colours march past Hitler, Berlin, *c.* 1936.

Massed standards and guidons on parade at Potsdam, 1937.

A Panzer II flying the regimental guidon leading a parade in Berlin shortly after the occupation of Austria, 1938.

clutching a black swastika. In each of the four corners was a swastika standing on its point. The flag was edged on the three flying sides by a double fringe of silver aluminium threads, 4.5 cm long.

The staff carrying the standard was twice the height of a man, and was topped by a spearpoint within which was an eagle carrying a swastika in its claws. Attached to the staff were streamers which indicated a special distinction for the unit, usually a battle honour. One unit whose colour was totally different from that described above was the 3rd Battalion of the 13th Grenadier Regiment, whose antecedents lay in the Austrian Imperial 'Hoch und Deutschmeister' Regiment.

Armoured units and other formations which were on Panzer division establishment or which had been horsed in former years, carried a guidon. This was a smaller version of the standard flag, and on its fly edge there was a 25 cm deep cut-out section which had the effect of making the fly edge a swallowtail. The staff bearing the guidon type of flag was unusual, in that the shaft was reinforced by six vertically placed, highly polished strips of metal, known as fillets, which encircled the whole shaft. The staff of the guidon was a single piece of oak, 3 m in length, painted black and varnished. Its head was a spearpoint made of highly polished aluminium, and was 28.6 cm in height. The Wehrmacht eagle within the spearhead was 11 cm in height.

The foot of the staff was capped with a 7 cm long deep brass ferrule which was

Adolf Hitler attending manoeuvres. The Führer Standard which marked his presence is carried by an NCO.

The Führer Standard being displayed during an inspection visit Hitler made to the Siegfried Line in 1939. Note the Standard Bearer's Badge displayed on the right sleeve of the NCO's tunic.

polished and silvered. Fitting round the top of the staff was a 5 cm high ring or collar of polished metal, on which was engraved the unit's name. There was a second ring at the top of the staff, to which any commemorative streamers were fitted.

There were several other pieces of uniform equipment associated with flags and standards, including a gorget suspended on a chain, which was worn by the NCO who carried the unit flag. During August 1936, a new pattern gorget was introduced. This was a metal plate of half-moon shape, carrying in the two upper corners a stud which held the chain. Each stud was embossed with an oak leaf cluster. In the centre of the gorget there was a Wehrmacht eagle set between two miniature facsimiles of a regimental colour. The NCO carrying the flag also had a distinctive arm shield of cloth set upon a coloured backing, woven into which were a pair of flags in the appropriate arm-of-service colour. The points of the flagstaffs on the

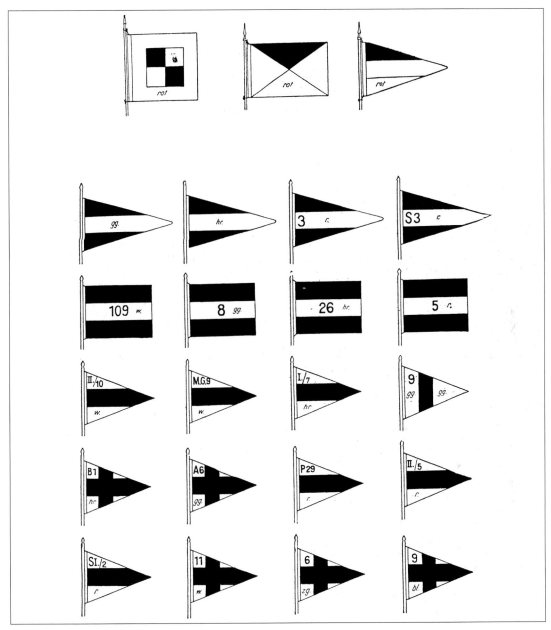

Flags of commanders and/or a unit headquarters. Top (left to right): the high command of an Army or an Army Group; the flag carried by a corps commander; the flag carried by a divisional commander. Lower levels of command, top (left to right): HQ of a cavalry brigade; HQ of an artillery commander; HQ of a Panzer brigade; HQ of a motorized rifle brigade. Second row: HQ of an infantry regiment; HQ of a cavalry regiment; HQ of an artillery regiment; HQ of a Panzer regiment. Third row: HQ of an infantry battalion; HQ of a machine gun battalion; HQ of an artillery battalion; HQ of the reconnaissance battalion of a division. Fourth row: HQ of an artillery observation battalion; HQ of a motorized reconnaissance battalion; HQ of a motorized anti-tank battalion; HQ of a motorized Panzer battalion. Bottom row: HQ of a rifle or motor cycle rifle battalion; HQ of a pioneer battalion; HQ of a signals battalion; HQ of a service corps unit.

Flags and standards of the Third Reich. Top: Standard of the Führer and Reichs Chancellor. Second row (left to right): the standard of the Supreme Commander of the Army; that of the Supreme Commander of the Luftwaffe; and that of the Supreme Commander of the Navy. Third row: the standard swastika banner; the Reichs War Flag; and the Reichs Service Flag.

arm badge pointed outwards, and set between them was a black Wehrmacht eagle holding a black swastika. Below this was a cluster of oakleaves.

The lined leather sash to carry the colour had a face which was bordered by two wide bands of silver aluminium braid, between which was a strip of cloth in arm-of-service colour. At the bottom of the sash was a carrying cup. The sash passed over the wearer's left shoulder, and was adjusted so that the cup was positioned on the right hip, just below the level of the waist belt. When the flag was carried, the bearer supported the

Heavy artillery driving past the reviewing stand, Nuremberg, 1938.

carrying cup with his right hand. His left arm passed horizontally across his chest to grasp the staff. The sash could be protected in inclement weather by a cover of artificial black leather. When the colour was not being paraded, it was protected by a covering of light muslin cloth. A foul-weather casing for the colour was made of black, waxed, waterproof cloth, which was topped by a metal cap.

The Führer's personal standard was a square of red-coloured cloth whose size depended upon the use to which it was being put. When mounted on a vehicle, for example, it was a 30 cm square piece of silk with silk thread or gold wire hand-embroidered decoration of a white disc, set inside which was a circular wreath of gold oak leaves bound at the four cardinal points with a gold ribbon. Inside the wreath was an upright black swastika, and in each corner of the red field was an eagle clutching in its claws a wreathed swastika. In the top right-hand corner and the lower left-hand corner, the eagle was the Nazi Party type, with the other two eagles being of Wehrmacht pattern, all four in gold. The standard was edged on all four sides with a double border of a wide black band and a narrow inner one in white.

The Minister of War, the Commander-in-Chief of the Wehrmacht, the Chief of the German Army and the Chief of the Army's General Staff also had flags which identified their appointments.

At a lower level, a pennant was carried on his car by a unit commander. A larger version of the same device, when fitted to a staff, marked that officer's headquarters. Examples of such pennants are shown on page 159.

CHAPTER THIRTEEN

UNIFORMS

Uniform, the clothing worn by military forces, is coloured to blend soldiers in with the surrounding terrain and thus partly camouflage them. Uniform also makes soldiers identifiable by their own Army, and distinguishes them from the enemy. In the German Army, Feldgrau, the shade of grey which had been the uniform colour since Imperial days, was changed during the Second World War to become a grey/green shade. Before the Nazi accession to power, the Army of the Weimar Republic wore the pattern of uniform which had been issued to the Imperial Army. The Nazi Party reintroduced conscription in 1935, and brought in a new pattern of military dress designed to raise the profile of the soldier. That uniform was smart and practical, and was issued in two types: dress was for ceremonial purposes, and service dress was

Soldiers of the Army of the Weimar Republic, seen here wearing the shoddy uniforms which were phased out in the first years of the Nazi regime.

The first winter of the war in Russia demonstrated that the Army was not prepared for the low temperatures and the biting cold. The Reichs government instituted a collection of warm clothing for issue to the front-line soldiers, and the wagon in this photograph is being emptied of the supplies it carried for them to be taken eastwards.

not only worn in barracks, but also doubled as combat uniform in time of war.

The basic uniform consisted of headdress, tunic or jacket, trousers and footwear. The German Army of the Hitler period had eight types of uniform, including sports gear, fatigue dress, field service, reporting and guard dress. The uniform for the last two was the standard service dress uniform embellished with certain additions. In parade dress and in walking out dress, the soldier wore an elaborately piped tunic.

This chapter will deal only with uniform worn by the rank and file. Officer-pattern clothing was similar to that of the other ranks, but made of finer cloth.

FOOTWEAR

Perhaps the best-known item of German military clothing was the jackboot – more correctly called a 'marching boot' (Marschstiefel). This type of footwear was made of black leather, and was worn by all units except those which were mounted. The Marschstiefel came up the leg to just below the knee, and thus kept the trouser bottoms dry and free from caked mud. The sole of the boot was heavily studded, and the heel was steel-tipped.

During the middle years of the war, supplies of leather began to run short, and as a replacement for Marschstiefel, lace-up boots with canvas anklets were tried in 1943, and

The 'Großdeutschland' Regiment had a specially designed uniform of the type worn by this soldier. The tunic was elaborately piped around the shoulder straps, collar, cuffs and front of the tunic, all in arm-of-service colour. The collar displays the type of Litzen worn in the Imperial Army to denote the Guards regiment.

then went into general issue. There were two other types of high boot which were produced to counter the wet and bitter cold conditions of the Eastern Front. One was a jackboot made with felt uppers and leather soles. Boots of this type were worn instead of the leather Marschstiefel. The other type was a large overboot made of plaited straw, inside which the boot fitted. A tropical variant of the jackboot was the lace-up canvas boot issued to German soldiers campaigning in North Africa. Soldiers of the Gebirgsjäger arm of service were issued with specially studded, ankle-high climbing boots (Bergschuhe). Cavalry units

had riding boots which came higher up the leg than the Marschstiefel. For physical training, cross-country running or similar occasions when the wearing of Marschstiefel would have been inappropriate, soldiers wore a soft, plimsoll-type of foot-covering (Laufschuhe).

TROUSERS

These were straight-legged, grey in colour, and unpiped except for those issued as part of parade dress. Parade dress trousers were also worn with walking out dress or for ceremonial occasions. Trousers of that pattern were piped down the outer seam of each leg in arm-of-service colour. Boots were worn with trousers – the wearing of shoes with trousers was expressly forbidden.

The trousers had a high waist, a four-button fly, and a fifth button to fasten the top of the trousers. There were two pockets at the hip, a pocket at the back, and a fob pocket at the front. There were buttons on the waistband to which cloth braces were attached.

Mounted units wore riding breeches, and Panzer troops were issued with full-length trousers gathered at the ankle, which fitted into lace-up ankle boots. Trousers for Panzer units were of black cloth, and were unpiped.

TUNICS

To replace the shabby Weimar jacket, the first tunic type was issued in 1936. This was single-breasted and fastened by five dull metal buttons down the front, and with another on each of the two hip and two breast pockets. The pockets were box-pleated and fitted with three-pointed flaps. The turn-down collar was faced with a dark-green cloth, and on either side of the collar join there was a patch (Litze) showing the arm-of-service colour. Dark-green cloth was also used as the backing for the national emblem (Hoheitsabzeichen), which was positioned above the right breast pocket, as

German Army despatch riders, wearing protective top coats, are seen in this photograph signalling to the vehicles in the column they are leading.

well as for the dark-green shoulder straps. The tunic fastened at the neck by a hook-and-eye fitting. In addition to the four external pockets, there was another inside the right-hand front of the tunic which carried field dressing.

The waist of the tunic had eyelet holes, two in the front of the garment and two at the back. Into these were fitted support hooks for the leather waist belt and the equipment which fitted onto it. The back skirt of the tunic had a 15 cm deep vent. The sleeves of other ranks' tunics had no turn-back cuff, but could be adjusted to fit tightly around the wrist. When worn as service dress, the jacket was buttoned up to the neck, but on the march or on active service, the top button and the hook-and-eye fitting were left unfastened.

In 1943, Germany's clothing factories began to run short of raw material, and this was reflected in a change to the 1936 pattern tunic. The dark-green collar and shoulder straps were replaced by field grey cloth, and pockets were no longer pleated. In the following year, there was an even more drastic change when the tunic with a skirt became a blouse, like the British Army's battle dress. At that time, the uniform colour also changed, as mentioned above, from field grey to a shade of grey-green. In the 1944 pattern blouses there was no tunic skirt, but instead a 12 cm deep waistband. The loss of the skirt meant that there were no longer two external hip pockets, but these were replaced by two pockets fitted inside the blouse. There was no pocket for field dressing.

Jackets and trousers in green/brown camouflage pattern were also issued for summer wear and for snipers, while in snowy conditions, white camouflage clothing was substituted. In addition, anoraks were issued for winter conditions, and in the middle years of the war, overalls were brought in which were reversible, and could show either summer or winter camouflage.

GREATCOATS

There were several styles on issue, but the standard one was of field grey with a dark-green collar, double-breasted, and worn by all ranks up to that of general, as well as by all arms of service. The greatcoat was long, reaching almost to the calves, was double-breasted, and fastened to the neck by two rows of six buttons. Men who had been awarded the Knight's Cross were allowed to wear their greatcoat collar open in order to display the decoration. Generals, too, wore their greatcoat open in order to show the red-coloured lapels of their rank. The garment had two 'slash' pockets set at an angle and fitted with rounded pocket flaps. Sleeves had a turn-back cuff, and the shoulders carried straps, which were worn by all ranks.

One variant issued during the war had a field grey collar, and a second had a larger than usual collar for foul-weather wear; a third had two extra side pockets, while the final variant had reinforced leather patches on the shoulders.

The 'Großdeutschland' Infantry Regiment had a specially designed pattern greatcoat, and the Africa Corps had one that was brown in colour. There were other overcoat patterns, for officers only, which were either in leather or were fur-lined.

HEADDRESS

The 'coal-scuttle' steel helmet was another piece of uniform which immediately identified the German soldier. The 1935 pattern, which was lighter and smaller than the 1916 pattern helmet, was itself replaced by the 1943 version, which was of very simple construction, being stamped out of a single piece of metal. Helmets were made in five basic sizes, and weighed 0.82 kg–1.2 kg. A special lightweight pattern in plastic was issued for wear by senior officers in parade dress. All helmets carried two small holes for ventilation, and were painted both internally and externally in field grey. In peacetime and for the first years of the war, each helmet carried a pair of decals. On

The German Army issued facial mosquito nets to units serving in theatres of war where there were biting insects, such as the desert, Finland or the high north. The nets were also a useful camouflage device. In this picture, the troops, both on the march and resting, have been issued with mosquito nets, but many are not wearing them.

the right side, there was a shield in the national colours of red, white and black; on the left side, a shield displaying the Wehrmacht eagle. The decals were discontinued during 1943. Light alloy decals had also been issued for wear on tropical helmets.

Inside the helmet there was a spring aluminium band, held in place by fittings at the rear and on both sides. The crown of the wearer's head was cushioned by a lining of thin leather, drawn together by a draw-string. The adjustable chinstrap was of black leather.

All ranks wore a peaked cap (Schirmmütze) with service, undress uniform and for walking out. The cap was worn in parade dress by officers and NCOs only. The Schirmmütze had a field grey top, a cap band of dark-green, and a shiny ridged peak. The rank and file had a black leather chinstrap, held in position by two black buttons. Officers wore a silver cord chinstrap, fastened by two silver buttons, and generals had gold fittings. The cap was piped in arm-of-service colours – except for generals – around the crown, as well as round the top and bottom edges of the coloured cap band. All Schirmmützen carried metal alloy versions of the national eagle and the national cockade surrounded by a wreath of oakleaves. Certain soldiers carried additional fittings: military chaplains, for example, had a small cross fitted between the eagle and the oakleaf wreath.

The field service cap (Feldmütze) came in various styles, and was worn by all ranks of the Army. The earliest other ranks pattern, the Model 38, was in field grey, and carried on the front an inverted chevron, piped in arm-of-service colour, and a cloth national emblem eagle was worn above the chevron. The model 1942 cap was similar in design to that of 1938, but did not carry the coloured chevron. Instead, it had two buttons at the front of the cap. There were two types of officers' field service caps, one of which was a variant of the officers' Schirmmütze, but without the cap cords, and with the national emblem and wreath of machined aluminium thread.

The year 1943 saw the introduction of the general-issue field cap (Einheitsmütze), based on the pattern of headdress worn by the Africa Corps. In field grey (black for Panzer troops), it carried the eagle emblem at the front of the cap, and the national cockade below this. The grey, cloth, semi-stiff peak was slightly longer than that of the Bergmütze worn by mountain troops. The front of the cap carried two grey buttons. Officers wore silver piping around the crown; generals wore gold. In winter conditions, there were fur caps of various patterns, as well as a field grey form of the British Army's cap-comforter.

COLOURS AND INSIGNIA

The uniform worn by Panzer crews was in black, so as not to show oil stains. The jacket was short and double-breasted, and normally worn open at the neck to show the grey shirt and a black tie. The wearing of arm-of-service pink piping around the jacket collar was discontinued in 1942, but was retained around the death's head patch on both lapels. The same pattern jacket was also worn by the crews of assault gun units, but in that case the colour was not Panzer black, but field grey.

The German Army was strongly colour-orientated, and used certain colours (known as Waffenfarben) to identify each arm of service. Other colours also identified a battalion or a company within a regiment. The basic Waffenfarben were:

White	Infantry
Light Green	All types of Jäger and also light infantry
Pink	Panzer
Black	Engineers
Golden yellow	Cavalry and reconnaissance troops
Lemon yellow	Signals
Bright red	Artillery
Carmine red	Generals in the high command
Cornflower blue	Medical staff

Arm-of-service colour piping was worn principally around the shoulder straps, but parade or full dress uniform also carried piping on other parts of the tunic, as well as the trousers. High command dress regulations laid down that in addition to the piping, a number, letter or device was to be worn on the shoulder strap as a further identification. In certain cases, all three were displayed. In addition to the arm-of-service piping, NCO shoulder straps bore 0.5 cm of silver lace stitched round the inner edge of the shoulder strap. Two strands of silver braid fitted close together formed the shoulder straps of subaltern officers. Field officers

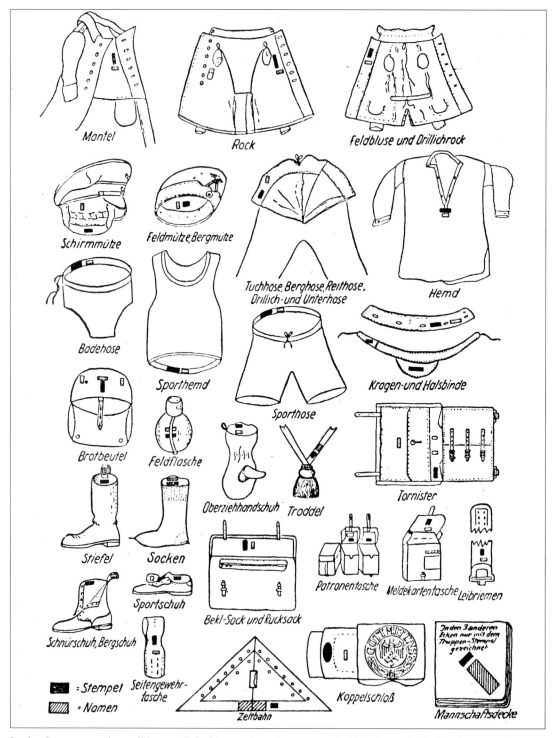

In the German services, all items of clothing and equipment carried labels marked with the wearer's name. The location of the tab which carried the name was laid down in regulations, and is shown coloured black in these drawings.

(ranks from major upwards) had a shoulder strap which was made of the same thickness of braid, but plaited to form five loops. A sixth loop of braid fastened around the button which held the shoulder strap in place. For ranks from major-general upwards, the cord was of interwoven gold and silver braid, and was plaited into five loops of braid, four of which rested on the shoulder, the fifth loop fitting around the shoulder strap button.

The metal shoulder strap button was in grey for other ranks, in silver for officers, and in gilt for generals. In addition to wearing a regimental or other identifying number on the shoulder strap, there were several Army formations which were authorized to wear special distinctive insignia, either on that strap, or else on the cap. Among those units was the 134th Grenadier Regiment, which displayed the cross of the 'Hoch und Deutschmeister Order' on its shoulder straps. The 'Großdeutschland' formations wore an alloy badge with the intertwined initials 'GD', while the Berlin and Vienna Guard Regiments displayed an alloy initial 'B' or 'W'. Units of the 'Feldherrenhalle' Division had on their shoulder straps the 'SA' rune, and the 'Führergrenadier' Battalion had the initials 'FG'. The use of permanently affixed numbers or numerals was discontinued during the middle years of the war, and these were replaced by slip-on titles of field grey cloth. Another device worn on the cap was the death's head, worn by the 5th Cavalry Regiment to commemorate the Prussian Guard Hussars whose traditions it continued. Another death's head device was that which had originally been carried by the 92nd Infantry Regiment (Braunschweig), and which was worn by the formation which had inherited its traditions. A third cap device was the Schwedter Adler, which had been carried by the 1st Brandenburg Dragoon Regiment. Mountain infantry units carried a metal Edelweiss.

As a further aid to identification, in addition to the coloured piping around the shoulder straps, all ranks below generals carried patches (Litzen) on their collars which displayed the Waffenfarbe.

Insignia showing that the wearer had a trade or was a specialist within his unit were worn only by the rank and file. Such devices

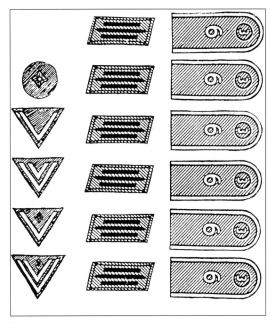

Junior ranks in the German Army carried their rank badges on the left sleeve. Ranks from corporal to field-marshal carried their rank distinctions on the shoulder boards of the tunic. Senior officers, that is those of general rank and above, also carried a stylized leaf design on either side of the collar join.
Schütze (Private): no chevron.
Oberschütze (Private First Class): one dull silver diamond.
Gefreiter (Lance-Corporal): one dull silver chevron.
Obergefreiter (Corporal) with fewer than six years' service: two dull silver chevrons.
Obergefreiter (Corporal) with more than six years' service: one dull silver chevron and one diamond.
Stabsgefreiter (Corporal on administrative duty): two dull silver chevrons and one diamond.

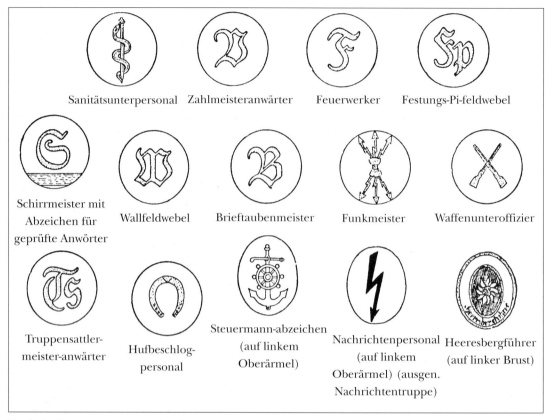

Sanitätsunterpersonal	Zahlmeisteranwärter	Feuerwerker	Festungs-Pi-feldwebel

Schirrmeister mit Abzeichen für geprüfte Anwörter   Wallfeldwebel   Brieftaubenmeister   Funkmeister   Waffenunteroffizier

Truppensattler-meister-anwärter   Hufbeschlog-personal   Steuermann-abzeichen (auf linkem Oberärmel)   Nachrichtenpersonal (auf linkem Oberärmel) (ausgen. Nachrichtentruppe)   Heeresbergführer (auf linker Brust)

Trade badges were worn on the sleeve only by other ranks. Top (left to right): Medical Orderly; Pay Corps; Weapons Artificer; Sergeant in a Fortress Pioneer Unit. Second row: Qualified Saddler; Sergeant in a Fortifications Unit; Carrier Pigeon NCO; Radio Operator; Corporal in an Ordnance Unit. Third row: Trainee as a Troop Saddler; Farrier; Helmsman in an Assault Boat (this badge was worn on the upper left arm); Signals Personnel; Army Mountain Guide (this badge was worn on the left breast).

were embroidered with the device in cotton or silk thread, or sometimes in silver wire. The most common insignia were the serpent staff of the medical corps, the lightning flash of the signals, the wheel of the transport personnel and the cogwheel of the Panzer repairmen. At a higher level than that of the individual soldier – at arm-of-service level – there were badges which indicated proficiency within that arm. These were awarded chiefly to Jäger, and included the Gebirgsjäger Edelweiss badge, which was worn on the upper right sleeve to show that the wearer was a qualified mountaineer. That sleeve badge was complemented by a metal Edelweiss worn on the left side of the peaked field cap. The ski-Jäger badge was another device worn on the arm and showed the oakleaves of the Jäger, upon which was superimposed a single ski. The Mountain Guide badge, awarded to Gebirgsjäger who had gained that high degree of proficiency, was of enamelled metal, and was worn on the left breast pocket. Mention is made in the

GENERAL OFFICERS

Company officers' insignia:

Leutnant (2nd Lieutenant): lowest-ranking officer. No stars on shoulder straps.

Oberleutnant (1st Lieutenant): shoulder strap has one gold star.

Hauptmann (Rittmeister in the cavalry) (Captain): two gold stars on shoulder straps.

Field officers' insignia:

Major (Major): shoulder strap has no star.

Oberstleutnant (Lieutenant-Colonel): one gold star on shoulder strap.

Oberst (Colonel): two gold stars on shoulder strap.

General officers' insignia:

Generalmajor (Major-General): no star on shoulder strap.

Generalleutnant (Lieutenant-General): one silver star.

General der Infanterie, etc. (General): two silver stars.

Generaloberst (Colonel-General): three silver stars.

Generalfeldmarschall (Field-Marshal): two crossed batons.

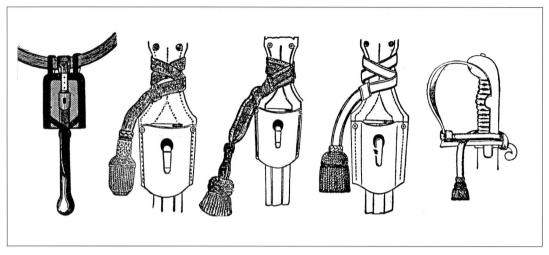

Left to right: the method of attaching the entrenching tool to the belt; the three ways in which the bayonet knot was tied for the various grades of NCOs; and the method in which a sword knot was tied.

section on flags that the NCO who carried the unit colour had a sleeve badge denoting his post, and a cloth badge was also worn on the upper left arm by members of the military field police.

Lanyards were worn by other ranks to indicate skill in marksmanship. These silver cords were fixed to the right shoulder by a toggle device, passed across the chest and fastened to the second button inside the tunic. The lanyard which was fastened to the right shoulder carried a silver alloy device of an eagle. Higher grades of marksmanship were denoted in the infantry by additional acorns suspended from the lanyard. For Panzer troops, the shield showed not an eagle, but a tank, and the various grades of proficiency for both Panzermen and artillerymen were signified by miniature shells instead of acorns.

Aigulettes were worn by all officers when wearing full dress, parade dress, walking out dress or on ceremonial occasions. For officers below the rank of general, those aigulettes were of plaited silver cording, and for generals, they were in gilt cord. The parade aigulette was worn around the right shoulder, and was carried across the right breast. It was held in place under the strap on the right shoulder by a small button, with the other end fastened by the second and third buttons of the tunic. The aigulette worn by *aides de camps* to indicate their office was of a simpler pattern, made of dull silver cord, and was worn on the tunic as well as the greatcoat.

Another example of the German Army's colour orientation was in the sidearm knots which were worn in peacetime, but which were discontinued during the war, except for soldiers stationed in the Homeland. Those types of decoration were known as Troddeln, Faustriemen or Portopée. The Troddel was worn on the sidearm by soldiers of the infantry, artillery, engineers and signals. Anti-tank units, cavalry and rifle regiments had Faustriemen.

The Troddel consisted of a support strap in dark cloth, a coloured slide showing the company colour, the shaft which carried the battalion colour, the crown which also displayed the company colour, and the tassel coloured to match the strap. The

Faustriemen, or wrist strap, differed only in that the strap was coloured field grey, the slide was in battalion colour, the crown in squadron colour, and the tassel in grey or green.

There were bayonet knots or Portopée of special pattern for NCOs and for those above the appointment of Fähnrich. When the Portopée was worn on the officer-pattern dagger, it was in silver, while that on the standard bayonet or sabre for NCOs was in field grey.

One of the most distinctive types of decoration worn on the tunic were cuff titles, awarded either to identify a unit or as the equivalent of a campaign decoration. The most widespread of the first type of titles were those worn by SS formations. Of the campaign bands, the best known was that for Africa, authorized on 18 July 1941, which had the words 'AFRIKA KORPS' picked out in silver block letters on a dark-green cloth background, and was edged at the top and bottom by a thin silver stripe. The band was carried on the right sleeve, unlike the later variant, which was worn on the left and carried the single word 'AFRIKA' set between two palm trees, and was of a cheaper design, silver-grey cotton thread substituting for the silver embroidery of the original. It was possible for both cuff titles to be worn.

The 3 cm wide cuff band 'KRETA' was issued to all those who had fought in the campaign on Crete in 1941, and consisted of that single word in yellow thread on a white cloth background set between two acanthus leaves in yellow cotton thread.

Other cuff titles issued during the war were for 'KURLAND' (Courland) to commemorate the battles fought in that area of Latvia. This cuff title was the last to be authorized in the war, and was instituted in March 1945, only weeks before the end of hostilities. It was worn on the left cuff. The cuff band 'METZ – 1944' recognized the part played in the defence of that city from July to September of that year. The band was worn on the left cuff.

Cuff titles for Army units were awarded to formations on the 'Großdeutschland' establishment and evolved out of the title carried by all ranks of the former Infantry Regiment 'Großdeutschland'. The regimental cuff band was of black cloth with silver characters in Gothic script and edged in silver thread. There was a later version which had a dark-green background. Both types of band were worn on the right cuff.

There were also cuff titles for the 'Brandenburg' Regiment (later a division), the 'Feldherrenhalle' formations, and for the 'List' Infantry Regiment as well as for all ranks of the 'Feldmarschall von Mackensen' Regiment. The Army personnel of Hitler's HQ carried a cuff title of black cloth, embroidered in gold with the word 'FÜHRERHAUPTQUARTIER' in Gothic letters with a gold edging. There were other cuff bands issued to minor units such as NCOs' schools, the Field Post Office and the Army propaganda units, as well as the Film Department.

Chapter Fourteen

Personal Equipment, Identity Documents and the Matter of Honour

Personal equipment

The basic equipment carried by German soldiers in the Second World War was of natural leather, which polishing soon discoloured black. The waist belt worn by other ranks was fastened by a square alloy buckle. On its face was carried an embossed Wehrmacht eagle, set inside a wreath of oak leaves. That wreath was surmounted by the motto 'Gott mit uns' (God [is] with us').

The waist belt supported all the other pieces of equipment worn by the soldier, the chief of which were six ammunition pouches, each of which contained two clips of five rounds of rifle ammunition. The pouches, which fitted three on each side of the buckle, had at their back a slide through which the belt passed. With the wider distribution of machine pistols, pouches to hold six magazines of machine pistol ammunition replaced those for the rifle rounds. The machine pistol pouches were also carried three on either side of the belt buckle, and each held a single magazine (37 rounds) of 9 mm ammunition. Unlike the rifle ammunition pouches, which were of leather, those for the machine pistol were of olive-green canvas.

On the left hip, the soldier carried a bayonet frog of leather. Into this fitted a black metal sheath enclosing the short 84/98 bayonet, which had a Bakelite grip. Also worn on the left hip was the entrenching tool (kleiner Spaten), a flat-bladed, short-handled shovel which was held in a canvas carrier. Regulations laid down that the bayonet and entrenching tool were to be attached to each other under active service conditions, in order to prevent them clashing and making unnecessary noise.

On the right hip was carried the bread bag (Brotbeutel). This held washing kit, knife, fork and spoon, the day's rations, and the soldier's field cap. Another item suspended from the belt was a water bottle and its drinking cup (Feldflasche and Trinkbecher). The water bottle had a 1 litre capacity, and was made of aluminium covered with felt, to reduce glare and reflection. The drinking cup was inverted over the mouth of the water bottle, and held in place by a strap. The mess tins (Kochgeschirr) were also of aluminium, and consisted of a deep container with a lid, which could be used either as a frying pan or as a plate. The mess tins were also held together by a leather strap, and were carried

Two views of the leather equipment worn by German servicemen. The left-hand photograph shows an Unteroffizier carrying the two adjustable front straps fastened to his waist belt. The right-hand picture shows the two straps fastening at the back to form a single support, the two carrying rings for the Rucksack, the large supporting hook at the back, the water bottle on the left side of the belt and the bread bag on the right.

either fastened to the small backpack (Sturmgepäck) or worn on the left hip. The Sturmgepäck was the equivalent of the British Army's 'battle order', and consisted of a few pieces of personal equipment which the soldier would need during the fighting and in the immediate post-battle period.

The waist belt could be fitted with leather braces (Koppelgestell), which supported the belt, the ammunition pouches, bread bag and water bottle. The braces consisted of a pair of straps at the front of the body which passed over the shoulders and joined at the back to form a single brace. At shoulder level on the front straps were two D-shaped rings, to which the various pieces of equipment or various types of pack could be fitted. The two front braces clipped onto

175

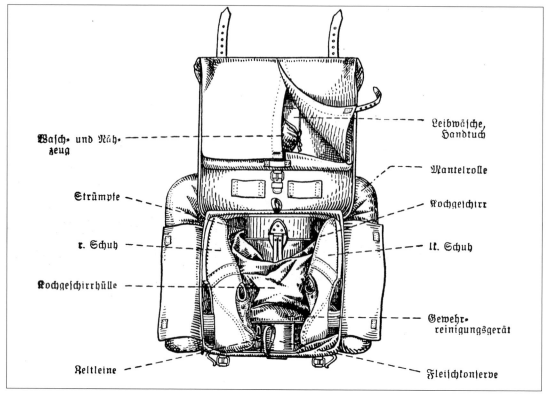

A drawing of the way in which a Rucksack was packed, showing the space for washing and sewing equipment at the top of the pack. In the lower half were carried socks, mess tins, boots, rifle cleaning kit, cans of meat and the two-tent cord, and the overcoat was carried rolled on the outside of the pack.

The shelter half, or Zeltbahn, was a waterproof garment which had several uses. One of these was to form an outer garment for the soldier in rainy weather. It was also used to construct a simple two-man tent, or with extra shelter halves, a larger tent capable of holding several soldiers.

The Zeltbahn could be utilized to make a tent big enough to hold eight soldiers, as shown here. This photograph has an interesting history. The film was in the camera of a German soldier killed in action on Crete, 1941. The New Zealand soldier who picked up the camera had the film developed, and it shows Fallschirmjäger in southern Greece preparing for the mission in Crete.

D-rings at the back of the ammunition pouches, and the single brace at the back was attached to the waist belt by a wide hook.

In addition to this basic equipment, a Rucksack of green canvas or a large, square-shaped pack (Tornister) of cow hide was issued. Both types of container were attached to the D-rings on the two front braces. The Tornister/Rucksack held spare clothing, as well as the pole sections and the two tent pegs used to set up a canvas shelter or two-man tent. This camouflaged shelter (Zeltbahn) also served as a waterproof cover for the soldier in foul-weather conditions.

A gas mask and container (Gasmaske and Tragbüchse) were carried on a strap, and rested on the left hip.

There were tropical variants of the leather equipment which were of green canvas.

IDENTITY DOCUMENTS

The more important of the two documents which were worn or carried at all times was the identity disc. This was 5 cm long and oval-shaped. Made of zinc, it was perforated, and had stamped into both halves the wearer's details, such as his name and the field post number which identified his parent unit or that of his replacement unit. In some cases, the zinc oval also carried the soldier's religion.

When the soldier was killed, the identity disc was snapped in two along the perforation, and the free half sent to the Army Records Department. The other half was left on the string around the dead soldier's neck, and was buried with him.

The second identity document was the Soldbuch: a record of the soldier's military and pre-military service, the courses he had

An NCO of the SS 'Leibstandarte Adolf Hitler' in parade uniform. Note the belt buckle, the cuff band and the way in which the sword knot was tied. The chevron on the right arm was not a rank distinction, but showed that he was a long-serving member of the SS.

undertaken, the decorations he had won, and injections he had been given. The inside front cover of the Soldbuch carried the soldier's photograph, his signature and service number.

The SS had an additional aid to identification. Aware that the underarm area usually survived the most severe wounding, the Waffen-SS authorities ordered that their soldiers be tattooed in that hollow. The tattoo showed the soldier's blood group, and often his service number. The practice of underarm tattooing fell into abeyance when service in the Waffen-SS was no longer by voluntary enlistment. It follows that foreign nationals were not tattooed.

THE MATTER OF HONOUR

Chapter Ten described the Army other ranks waist-belt buckle, but since the text of this book includes both paratroops and the Waffen-SS, mention must be made of the pattern of belt buckle worn by other ranks of those arms of service.

The paratroop belt buckle displayed an oval wreath, within which was a free-flying eagle. No legend was carried on the buckle, but that worn by other ranks of the Waffen-SS was embossed with a stylized Nazi Party-type eagle, whose outstretched wings surmounted a wreath carrying the legend 'Meine Ehre heißt Treue' ('Loyalty is my honour').

Honour was a matter which was not taken lightly in the German services. During the years of the Third Reich, the parade at which a recruit took the oath of allegiance was as solemn an affair as it had been under the Kaiser. During the years of the Weimar Republic, it had lost its almost religious significance, but during the government by the Nazi Party, the emphasis on loyalty and honour was restored and even accentuated. The wording of the oath taken by recruits during the Hitler years was:

I swear by God this sacred oath: I will render unconditional obedience to Adolf Hitler, the Führer of the Reich, Supreme Commander of the Armed Forces, and shall at all times be prepared as a brave soldier to give my life for this oath.

Recruits in a Gebirgsjäger unit, seen here taking the oath of allegiance on the regimental colour.

Recruits of an infantry regiment taking the oath of allegiance. The tribune is decorated with the Reichskriegflagge.

The last pre-war swearing in of recruits to the SS VT Division, East Prussia, August 1939.

Because this oath was a commitment made by each soldier to the Führer, and because of its personal nature, it could not be lightly broken, and this is why senior officers of the Army found it almost impossible to act treasonably against Hitler: their code of honour would not permit it. Nor was that attitude towards honour confined just to officers of high rank. Soldiers of the rank and file who had been court-martialled for military offences were grouped into a special division, the 999th, where they could redeem their military honour by undertaking unusually dangerous tasks. There is an authenticated report of a soldier of the 999th who acted bravely during one American attack in Tunisia, and who was then heard to declare: 'Sergeant, I don't care what happens to me now. I have redeemed my military honour.' To that man, as to the millions of Germans who fought in the war, his honour as a soldier was an affair of the greatest importance.

Chapter Fifteen

Medals and Decorations

It was not usual for the German armed forces to issue campaign medals. Instead, they produced a variety of devices to be worn on the tunic, and these included awards for bravery and for participation in a campaign. The most common of the various metal or cloth distinctions are described below.

The Iron Cross (Das Eiserne Kreuz)

Originally a Prussian decoration, this did not become a German one until the outbreak of the Second World War. The Iron Cross was instituted at the outbreak of each national war: 1813, 1870, 1914 and 1939.

For the war years of 1813, 1870 and 1914, there were only two classes of cross, the Second and First, although a special Grand Cross could be awarded. In 1939, the number of classes was increased from two to three by the inclusion of the Knight's Cross, and at various times during the war, additions were made which upgraded the level of that cross. The first of these was an oakleaf cluster, then the oakleaf cluster with swords, thirdly the addition of diamonds to the oakleaf cluster and swords, and finally, the golden oakleaf cluster with swords and diamonds. During the war, a Grand Cross of the Iron Cross was instituted and bestowed upon Hermann Goering, the Commander-in-Chief of the Luftwaffe. The golden oakleaf cluster was also awarded only once: to Colonel Rudel, commander of the Luftwaffe's 'Immelmann' Squadron.

All classes of the Iron Cross were of blackened metal with a silver edging. Both the obverse and the reverse carried motifs and/or dates. On the obverse of the Second World War Iron Cross was a swastika, and on the reverse the date 1813, commemorating the year in which the cross was first instituted. The ribbon upon which the cross was suspended was in the German national colours: black, white and red. The ribbon of the Second Class Cross was fitted into a buttonhole on the tunic, and was tucked inside the front edge so that the metal cross did not show. The First Class Cross had no ribbon, but was pinned onto the left breast pocket of the tunic.

The Knight's Cross was on a wider ribbon than that of the Second Class grade, and fastened round the neck. The additions to the Knight's Cross – the oakleaf cluster and the swords – were carried mounted on the upper arm of the Mantua-type cross.

The War Service Cross (Das Kriegsverdienstkreuz)

Hitler was aware that although there were circumstances and actions which merited a decoration, there was no civilian award for

Orders and medals of the German services. Top (left to right): First Class Iron Cross of the Great War (the Second Class Iron Cross of the Great War was worn suspended from a black and white ribbon); The Pour le Mérite; The Military Service Cross. Second row: Wounded badge of the First World War (in black for a single or a second wound, in silver for a third or fourth wound, in gold for five wounds or more); Golden Party Badge of the Nazi Party; the Blood Order, commemorating the abortive Putsch of 9 November 1923. Third row: Long Service Award (First Class in gold for 25 years' service; in silver for 18 years' service); Service Medal for 12 years' service (in bronze and matt silver for 4 years' service), Cross of Honour for front-line soldiers (for those who did not serve at the front, the cross was without swords). Bottom row: Medal for the Anschluß with Austria; Medal for the occupation of Czechoslovakia (with a bar for participation in the occupation of Bohemia and Moravia); The Cross of Honour for those who took part in the war in Spain.

Orders and medals of the German Services in the Second World War. Top (left to right): Iron Cross Second class; Iron Cross First class; Knight's Cross of the Iron Cross. Second row: War Service Cross with swords, First class (the Cross was coloured silver); when awarded without swords, it was given for non-combatant services; Grand Cross of the Iron Cross (awarded to Hermann Goering); War Service Cross with swords, Second class (in bronze). Bottom: The bar to the First class Iron Cross awarded during the First World War; bar to the Second class Iron Cross awarded during the First World War; Wounded badge.

The War Service Cross (Kriegsverdienstkreuz) was awarded to those soldiers and civilians for whom the award of the Iron Cross would have been inappropriate. In the Army, it was usually given for service in rear-area (non-combatant) units.

conspicuous service. He therefore instituted the War Service Cross on 18 October 1939. This award could be made with swords, for exceptional service conducted in the face of the enemy, or without swords for wartime duties which were not carried out on the field of battle, such as work in a factory producing armaments.

The Kriegsverdienstkreuz, in the shape of a Maltese cross, had three classes. The bronze Second Class was suspended on a ribbon which was worn in the fashion of the ribbon of the Second Class Iron Cross. The First Class War Service Cross was in silver, and was worn pinned to the left breast pocket. It had no ribbon. The Knight's Cross, a larger version of the First Class Cross, was worn on a wide ribbon which passed round the neck.

The obverse of the Second and First Class crosses carried the date '1939', surrounded by

a stylized laurel wreath. The reverse was plain. For those crosses which were issued 'with swords', a pair of crossed swords with points uppermost was displayed between the uppermost arms of the cross. The ribbon for the Second Class and for the Knight's Cross was in the German national colours: red, white and black, with the black central section being double the width of the red and white stripes.

On 19 August 1940, a War Service Medal was instituted. This was in bronze, and was worn on a ribbon of red, white and black, the latter bisected by a very thin red stripe. The obverse of the medal displayed the War Service Cross, and the reverse bore the words, 'For War Service', together with the date '1939'.

THE GERMAN CROSS (DAS DEUTSCHE KREUZ)

This award was instituted by Adolf Hitler on 28 September 1941 to reward war service, and was bestowed in one of two classes: Gold, for frequent examples of bravery in the face of the enemy, and Silver, for repeated outstanding examples of service in the leadership of troops.

The German Cross was worn on the right breast, and was an eight-pointed star in black and silver, whose central section, bearing the date '1941', was encircled by a laurel wreath in either gold or silver, according to class. The German Gold Cross carried an Iron Cross within a gold wreath, while the Silver award showed a War Service Cross with swords.

THE EAST FRONT MEDAL

'MEDAILLE WINTERSCHLACHT IM OSTEN 1941–42' OR 'OSTFRONTMEDAILLE'

This was one of the very few medals issued to commemorate a campaign. Another was the 'Errinerungsmedaille für den italienisch-deutschen Feldzug in Afrika' ('Commemorative

The medals, decorations and awards won by Paratrooper Adi Strauch. From top to bottom, they are: in the blue box, the Luftwaffe Paratroop qualifying badge; in the centre the Iron Cross Second Class, and below it the German Cross in Gold; on the right in the white-lined box, the Iron Cross First Class. The top cuff title is that of the 'Feldherrenhalle' Division, with which Strauch served for a short time. Below that, the 'Kreta' armband awarded for service in the campaign for Crete. The green cuff title is the unit one, in Strauch's case the 2nd Para Regiment. The silver badge on the left (crossed bayonet and grenade) is the general assault badge; that in the middle is the close combat award, then the badge issued by the Luftwaffe to its troops who took part in ground fighting. The last line of awards shows (left to right) the Wounded Badge in black, the pair of shoulder boards denoting Strauch's rank as a Sergeant, the silver/white cord below the star on

the shoulder board indicates that he was an officer cadet, and he was, in fact, commissioned late in 1944. The red ribbon on the extreme right carried the medal awarded for service on the Eastern Front, 1941. The arrowed insignia at the bottom is a Nazi Party award.

Medal for the Italo-German Campaign in Africa'). This decoration ceased to be worn after Italy left the Axis and surrendered.

The East Front Medal was instituted by Hitler on 26 May 1942, and was awarded to all ranks who had fought on the Eastern Front throughout the first winter campaign of 1941/2. The qualifying period was 15 November 1941 to 15 April 1942, but those dates were subsequently extended. The medal only ceased to be awarded on 4 September 1944, and the last bestowals were made on 15 October 1944.

The areas of operations within which the medal could be won were limited to east of the Ukraine or east of the Russo-Finnish border of 1940. For it to be awarded, the recipient had to have fought for two weeks,

or to have been wounded. Awards were made retrospectively for those who had been killed in action or who were listed as missing.

The circular-shaped medal carried on its top a miniature steel helmet of German pattern. Above that there was a carrying ring which held the medal ribbon. This was mainly red in colour, with three thin stripes: two in white, and a central one in black. Unless otherwise stipulated, the medal was represented either by a ribbon worn diagonally through the second buttonhole of the tunic – as is the case of the Second Class Iron Cross – or on a ribbon bar on the left breast.

An unusual fact about the East Front Medal was that although it was only a campaign medal, it took precedence over the War Service Medal.

CUFF BANDS AND TITLES

One of the most distinctive types of decoration were cuff titles, which were displayed either to identify the wearer's unit or to reward his service in a campaign. The most widespread use of the first, or unit, type was by the SS formations. Of the second, or campaign cuff bands, the best known are those for Africa and for Crete.

AFRIKA

This band, authorized on 18 July 1941, had the words 'AFRIKA KORPS' picked out in silver block letters on a dark-green cloth background, and was edged at the top and bottom by a thin silver stripe. The Afrika Korps band was carried on the right cuff, unlike a later variant which was worn on the left. That variant carried the single word 'AFRIKA' set between two palm trees worked in silver-grey cotton thread. It was possible for both cuff titles to be worn.

KRETA

This was a 3 cm wide band, and was issued to all those who had fought in the campaign on Crete in 1941. The cuff band displayed the single word 'KRETA' in yellow thread on a white cloth background, set between two acanthus leaves, which were also worked in yellow cotton thread.

Other cuff titles included 'KURLAND' (Courland) to commemorate the battles fought in that area of Latvia. This was the last cuff title to be authorized and was instituted in March 1945, only weeks before the end of the hostilities. It was worn on the left cuff.

The cuff band 'METZ 1944' recognized the part played in the defence of that city from July to September of that year. It was worn on the left cuff.

Unit cuff titles included that for the 'Großdeutschland' units. This was of black cloth with the title 'GROßDEUTSCHLAND' and an edging in silver thread. A later version had a dark-green, not a black background.

Both types of cuff band were worn on the right sleeve.

There were also cuff titles for the 'Brandenburg' Regiment (later a division), the 'Feldherrenhalle' formations, as well as for the infantry regiments 'List' and 'Feldmarschall von Mackensen'. Army personnel in Hitler's headquarters carried a black cloth title embroidered in gold with the word 'FÜHRERHAUPTQUARTIER' and edged with gold thread. There were also other cuff bands issued to such units as schools for NCOs, the Field Post Office and for Army propaganda units.

ARM SHIELDS

Among the more unusual types of battle badge were arm shields, instituted at various times during the war. These were worn on the upper left arm, either with or without a backing cloth. It was possible for a serviceman to gain more than one shield, and in such cases the earliest award was worn above the others.

In order of date, these shields were warded for the following campaigns.

NARVIK

Instituted on 19 August 1940 to commemorate the fighting for and the capture of the Norwegian port, it was awarded to all members of the armed forces who had taken part in the fighting between 9 April and 9 June.

The Army award was in grey metal, mounted on a grey backing.

CHOLM

Between 21 January and 5 May 1942, a small German garrison of some 5,000 men defended the small town of Cholm on the Lovat river, about 85 km north of Velikie Luki in the Kalinin region of Russia.

The shield was authorized on 1 July 1942, and was awarded to all the soldiers who had served in the encircled forces area, as well as to the aircrews who had landed on the small airstrip to supply the garrison.

The shield was in white metal, and had no backing cloth.

CRIMEA

This was instituted on 25 July 1942, and was to be awarded to all members of the armed forces who had been engaged in the fighting between 21 September 1941 and 4 July 1942.

The bronze-coloured shield was mounted on a cloth backing.

DEMJANSK

This was instituted on 25 April 1943, for all the men who had taken part in the fourteen-month-long siege of Demjansk, a small town lying between Novgorod and Velikie Lukie.

The shield was in white metal, and had no backing cloth.

KUBAN

Instituted on 20 September, and awarded to all those who had been engaged in the defensive fighting in the Kuban bridgehead from 1 February, 1943.

The bronze shield was on a cloth backing.

Several shields were proposed which did not go into official production.

WARSAW

This was intended to commemorate the part played by members of the armed forces and non-military personnel in the fighting in Warsaw between 1 August and 2 October 1944, but an air raid destroyed the dies from which the shields were to be cast, and no official ones were produced and issued.

LORIENT

The garrison of the U-boat base at Lorient held out to the end of the war, and to commemorate their resistance, they produced their own shield. Several patterns are known

to exist, in white metal, copper, aluminium, and even cloth when stocks of metal ran out.

LAPPLAND

This award was instituted in March 1945, so late in the war that only a few issues were made to members of the 20th (Gebirgs) Army, and it is surprising that even after the end of the war, the shield continued to be made and awarded.

BADGES FOR BRAVERY IN COMBAT

THE INFANTRY ASSAULT BADGE

This oval white metal badge was instituted on 20 December 1939. Originally intended for the infantry and mountain infantry arms of service, the conditions of award later included motorized infantry, whose badge was in bronze.

All ranks were eligible to receive the assault badge, which consisted of an oval of oakleaves, bound at the bottom. Lying diagonally across the wreath was a rifle and fixed bayonet, and at the top of the wreath was a Wehrmacht eagle holding a swastika.

To be awarded the badge, the recipient had to have taken part in at least three infantry attacks or counter-attacks on separate days. The badge was carried on the left breast pocket.

THE PANZER ASSAULT BADGE

This award, like that of the infantry, dated from 20 December 1939. The same conditions applied: three engagements with the enemy on different days. Originally awarded only to Panzer crews, the issue was extended on 1 June 1940 to embrace Panzer-grenadiers. For Panzer personnel, the badge colour was silver, but for Panzergrenadiers it was in bronze.

During 1942, there was a modification to the design of the badge, with the addition of the numbers '25', '50', '75' or '100', to indicate the number of days of battle in which the recipient had taken part.

The face of the German soldier towards the end of the war. This Unteroffizier is wearing above his right breast pocket a Close Combat Badge in silver, and on his right sleeve two silver stripes, each denoting an enemy tank destroyed in close combat.

The design and size of the '25' and '50' badges for Panzer crews differed from the '75' or '100'. The '25' and '50' badges had a tank in black set within a silver wreath with a silver eagle and swastika, while those for the '75' and '100' were larger in size, and had a gilt Panzer within a gilt wreath. For recipients other than Panzer crews, the badge was completely bronze for the '25' and '50' classes, and in bronze with a gilt wreath for the '75' and '100'.

The Panzer assault badge was worn on the left breast pocket, and only one award could be worn at any one time.

THE GENERAL ASSAULT BADGE

When introduced on 1 June 1940, this badge was worn as the Pionier Sturm Abzeichen (Assault Engineer Badge), but was later extended to include all fighting personnel who were not eligible for either the infantry or the Panzer battle badge. The condition of the award was that the recipient had to have taken part in three assaults on separate days. In June 1943, the design of the badge was changed to show the number of assaults which had been made, similar to the other battle badges.

The original badge was in silver-coloured metal, with the addition of the numbers '25' and '50' with a black eagle, bayonet and grenade set within a silver wreath, while the '75' and '100' carried a gilt wreath.

The device was worn on the left breast pocket.

Vinzenz Kaiser, carrying on his right sleeve the badges he had been awarded for the single-handed destruction of enemy tanks. One badge was awarded for each tank destroyed.

This was the end for over a million German soldiers: an isolated grave in a foreign country. In this photograph, the dead men are buried in a communal grave, with an escort of their own comrades.

THE CLOSE COMBAT CLASP

In 1942, it was realized that a new award was necessary to honour those infantry soldiers who had taken part in hand-to-hand fighting during which they were unsupported by armour. Although originally intended for infantry soldiers, other units were later made eligible. Hitler considered the gilt Close Combat Clasps to be of such importance that he intended to present them in person, and he made the first awards of that grade on 27 August.

The clasps was in three grades: bronze for 15 days of close combat, silver for 30 days, and gilt for 50 days.

The clasp was worn above the left breast pocket.

THE SPECIAL AWARD FOR SINGLE-HANDED DESTRUCTION OF A TANK

Although this device was authorized on 9 March 1942, its award was made retrospective to cover such actions since the first days of the invasion of the Soviet Union

in June 1941. It was intended as a reward for the *single-handed* destruction of an enemy tank, so that members of an anti-tank gun crew were not eligible.

The badge, of stiff silver cloth edged in black, was worn on the upper right arm, and carried in its centre a metal facsimile of a Soviet T 34 tank. One cloth badge was worn for each tank destroyed, and badges for subsequent victories were worn one above the other on the right arm. A gilt tank sleeve badge was instituted on 18 December 1943 to commemorate a fifth victory. That cloth badge had a gold tank facsimile, and also an edging in gold.

OTHER DECORATIONS

Other badges included the Army Flak Badge, a Balloon Observer's Badge, as well as a sleeve device, similar to that for the single-handed destruction of an enemy tank, but awarded for shooting down low-flying aircraft. There was also a cloth sleeve badge awarded to snipers.

APPENDIX I

COMPARATIVE TABLES OF RANK

British Army	German Army	Waffen-SS
Private, Gunner, Sapper, etc.	Grenadier, Kanonier, etc.	SS Grenadier, etc.
Lance-Corporal	Gefreiter	SS Sturmmann
Corporal	Obergefreiter	SS Rottenführer
Sergeant	Unteroffizier, etc.	SS Unterscharführer
Warrant Officer Class 2, Class 1	Feldwebel, Oberfeldwebel	SS Oberscharführer
2nd Lieutenant	Leutnant	SS Untersturmführer
Lieutenant	Oberleutnant	SS Obersturmführer
Captain	Hauptmann	SS Hauptsturmführer
Major	Major	SS Sturmbannführer
Lieutenant-Colonel	Oberstleutnant	SS Obersturmbannführer
Colonel	Oberst	SS Standartenführer
Brigadier	——	SS Oberführer
Major-General	Generalmajor	SS Brigadeführer
Lieutenant-General	Generalleutnant	SS Gruppenführer
General	General der Infanterie, etc.	SS Obergruppenführer
	Generaloberst	SS Obergruppenführer
Field-Marshal	Generalfeldmarschall	SS Oberstgruppenführer

(There were a number of ranks for which no British Army equivalents exist: these were for officer cadets in both the German Army and the SS.)

APPENDIX II

DIVISIONS OF THE WAFFEN-SS

1st SS Panzer Division 'Leibstandarte Adolf Hitler'
2nd SS Panzer Division 'Das Reich'
3rd SS Panzer Division 'Totenkopf'
4th SS Police Panzergrenadier Division
5th SS Panzer Division 'Wiking'

Reichspropagandaminister Joseph Goebbels (1897–1945), seen here with highly decorated officers of the Army. To keep himself in touch with current military developments, Goebbels regularly invited such men to discuss with him not only their achievements, but also the problems they were facing in the field.

Oberstgruppenführer Josef 'Sepp' Dietrich (1892–1966) commanded Hitler's SS Leibstandarte, or bodyguard, and rose to command the division which evolved from it. He then raised and commanded the 1st SS Panzer Corps and finally the 6th SS Panzer Army. Sentenced as a war criminal to twenty-five years imprisonment, he was released in 1959.

6th SS Gebirgs Division 'Nord'
7th SS Freiwilligen Gebirgs Division 'Prinz Eugen'
8th SS Cavalry Division 'Florian Geyer'
9th SS Panzer Division 'Hohenstaufen'
10th SS Panzer Division 'Frundsberg'
11th SS Freiwilligen Panzergrenadier Division 'Nordland'
12th SS Panzer Division 'Hitler Jugend'
13th Waffen Gebirgs Division der SS 'Handschar' (Kroatischen No. 1)
14th Waffen Grenadier Division der SS (Galisische No. 1)
15th Waffen Grenadier Division der SS (Lettische No. 1)
16th SS Panzergrenadier Division 'Reichsführer SS'
17th SS Panzergrenadier Division 'Goetz von Berlichingen'
18th SS Freiwilligen Panzergrenadier Division 'Horst Wessel'
19th Waffengrenadier Division der SS (Lettische No. 2)
20th Waffengrenadier Division der SS (Estnische No. 1)
21st Waffengebirgs Division der SS 'Skanderbeg' (Albanian No. 1)
22nd SS Freiwilligen Cavalry Division
23rd Waffengebirgs Division der SS 'Kama' (Kroatischen No. 2)

Field-Marshal Gunther von Kluge (1892–1944)
commanded the 4th Army in Poland and France,
and then took over Army Group Centre in Russia
in December 1941. He was invalided out of the
service following a car accident, but was recalled
to duty in 1944 as successor to Field-Marshal
Rommel as Commander of Army Group B.
Kluge committed suicide in 1944.

Sturmbannführer Otto Skorzeny, leader of
German command formations towards the
end of the war.

24th Waffengebirgs 'Karstjäger' Division der SS
25th Waffengrenadier Division der SS 'Hunyadi' (Ungarischen No. 1)
26th Waffengrenadier Division der SS (Ungarischen No. 2)
27th SS Freiwilligen Grenadier Division 'Langemarck'
28th SS Freiwilligen Panzergrenadier Division 'Wallonien'
29th Waffengrenadier Division der SS (Italienische No. 1)
30th Waffengrenadier Division der SS (Russische No. 2)
31st SS Freiwilligen Grenadier Division

Otto Skorzeny led a commando group which captured the Hungarian seat of power and kept that country in the war on Germany's side. Skorzeny, the tall, burly figure, is here seen with his officers on Castle Hill in Budapest immediately after the palace was taken.

32nd SS Freiwilligen Grenadier Division '30 January'
33rd Waffengrenadier Division der SS 'Charlemagne' (Französische No. 1)
34th SS Grenadier Division 'Landstorm Nederland'
35th SS Polizeigrenadier Division
36th Waffengrenadier Division der SS
37th SS Freiwilligen Kavallerie Division 'Luetzow'
38th SS Panzergrenadier Division 'Nibelungen'

There had been an intention to raise a Waffengrenadier Division der SS (Russische No. 1) which was to carry the number 29. This formation grew out of a self-help defence organization formed by a Pole, Bronislav Kaminski. The brutality of Kaminski's men was such that he was shot by the SS and his unit disbanded. The number 29 was then given to the Waffengrenadier Division der SS (Italienische No. 1).

Appendix III

Order of Battle –
Poland, September 1939

Army Group North (von Bock)

3rd Army (von Kuechler)

I Corps
11th and 61st Infantry Divisions; Armoured Battle Group 'Kempf'; 127th Infantry Division in reserve

Wodrig Corps
1st and 2nd Infantry Divisions

XXI Corps
21st and 28th Infantry Divisions

Brand Corps
Frontier Defence battalions and a cavalry brigade; 206th Infantry Division in reserve

4th Army

II Corps
31st and 32nd Infantry Divisions

III Corps
50th Division and Battle Group 'Netze'

XIX Panzer Corps (Guderian)
2nd and 20th Motorized Divisions; 3rd Panzer Division; 23rd, 73rd and 218th Infantry Divisions; 10th Panzer Division in reserve

Army Group South (von Rundstedt)

8th Army (Blaskowitz)

X Corps
24th, 30th and 183rd Infantry Divisions

XIII Corps
10th and 17th Infantry Divisions; SS (Motorized) Infantry Regiment 'Leibstandarte'

10th Army (von Reichenau)

XI Corps
18th and 19th Infantry Divisions

XIV Motorized Corps
13th and 29th Motorized Divisions

XV Motorized Corps
2nd and 3rd Light Divisions; 27th and 68th Infantry Divisions in reserve

XVI Panzer Corps
1st and 4th Panzer Divisions; 14th and 31st Infantry Divisions

IV Corps
4th and 6th Infantry Divisions; 62nd Infantry Division in reserve

Through periscope binoculars, Hitler observes the bombardment of Warsaw, Poland, 1939.

14TH ARMY (LIST)

VIII Corps
8th and 28th Infantry Divisions; 5th Panzer
Division and SS 'Germania' Regiment

XVII Corps
1st, 2nd and 3rd Mountain Divisions

XXII Panzer Corps
2nd Panzer and 4th Light Divisions

Hitler discusses the outcome of military
manoeuvres, 1938.

APPENDIX IV

ORDER OF BATTLE – THE WEST, 1940

ARMY GROUP B (VON BOCK)

18TH ARMY (VON KUECHLER) AND 6TH ARMY (VON REICHENAU)

XVI Panzer Corps (Hoepner)
3rd and 4th Panzer Divisions

XXXIX Panzer Corps (Schmidt)
9th Panzer Division

ARMY GROUP A (VON RUNDSTEDT)

4TH ARMY (KLUGE), 12TH ARMY (LIST) AND 16TH ARMY (BUSCH)

XV Panzer Corps (Hoth)
5th and 7th Panzer Divisions

XLI Panzer Corps (Reinhardt)
6th and 8th Panzer Divisions

XIX Panzer Corps (Guderian)
1st, 2nd, and 10th Panzer Divisions; Motorized Infantry Regiment 'Großdeutschland'

Colonel-General Hermann Hoth was born in 1895 and commanded a Panzer Corps during the French campaign. He then led Panzer Group 3 until he took over 17th Army. On 1 June 1942, he commanded Panzer Army 4, and retired from active service on 15 September 1942. Hoth was recalled to service in 1945 to take part in the final defence of the Reich. In October 1948, he was sentenced to fifteen years' imprisonment for war crimes.

Guderian and his staff at a roadside conference during the advance into Russia in the first year of the war against the Soviet Union, 1941.

XIV Motorized Corps (von Wietersheim)
Panzer Battalion No. 114; Panzergrenadier Regiments Nos 11 and 53

ARMY GROUP C (VON LEEB)

There were no armoured formations serving with either of the two Armies of this Army group: 1st (Blaskowitz) or 7th (Dollmann).

Appendix V

Order of Battle –
The Soviet Union, June 1941

ARMY GROUP NORTH (VON LEEB)

16TH ARMY (BUSCH) AND 18TH ARMY (KUECHLER)

4th Panzer Group
XLI Panzer Corps (Reinhardt): 1st and 6th Panzer Divisions; 36th Motorized Division
LVI Corps (von Manstein): 8th Panzer and 3rd Motorized Divisions; SS Division 'Totenkopf' in reserve

ARMY GROUP CENTRE (VON BOCK)

4TH ARMY (VON KLUGE) AND 9TH ARMY (STRAUSS)

2nd Panzer Group (Guderian)
XXIV Corps (von Schweppenburg): 3rd and 4th Panzer Divisions; 10th Motorized and 1st Cavalry Divisions
XLVII Panzer Corps (Lemelsen): 17th and 18th Panzer Divisions; 29th Motorized Division
XLVI Panzer Corps (von Vietinghoff): 10th Panzer Division; 'Das Reich' Division; 'Großdeutschland' Infantry Regiment

Field-Marshal von Leeb, who commanded Army Group North in Russia until he was dismissed by Hitler because of the failure of his troops to withstand the Red Army's offensive.

Above: Hitler and General (later Field-Marshal) Busch at a parade to mark the end of the war with Poland.

Right: General Heinz Guderian (1888–1954), here seen wearing the Knight's Cross with oakleaf. Guderian commanded XIX Corps in the Polish and French campaigns, and went on to lead Panzer Group 2 in Russia. He was relieved of his command at the end of 1941 for disobeying Hitler's order not to retreat. Circumstances forced Hitler to re-employ him in 1943, first as Inspector of Panzer Troops, and then, in 1944, as Army Chief of Staff. He was finally dismissed by Hitler on 28 March 1945.

3rd Panzer Group (Hoth)

XLIX Panzer Corps (Schmidt): 7th and 20th Panzer Divisions; 10th and 14th Motorized Divisions

LVII Panzer Corps (Kuntzen): 12th and 19th Panzer Divisions; 18th Motorized Division

ARMY GROUP SOUTH (VON RUNDSTEDT)

17TH ARMY (STULPNAGEL), 6TH ARMY (VON REICHENAU) AND 11TH ARMY (VON SCHOBERT)

1st Panzer Group (von Kleist)

III Panzer Corps (von Mackensen): 13th and 14th Panzer Divisions; SS 'Leibstandarte' and 'Wiking' Divisions

XIV Panzer Corps (von Wietersheim): 9th and 16th Panzer Divisions; 16th Infantry Division; 25th Motorized Division in reserve

General von Vietinghoff-Scheel, commander of an Army in Italy.

Field-Marshal Ewald von Kleist (1881–1954). He served in the French and Balkan campaigns, and advanced into the Caucasus during the 1942 summer campaign. He was taken prisoner by the British, who then handed him over to the Russians. Kleist died in a Soviet prison camp in 1954.

Hasso von Manteuffel (hands in pockets) and officers of the 'Großdeutschland' Division during operations on the Eastern Front, 1944–5, when Manteuffel was the Divisional Commander.

APPENDIX VI

ORDER OF BATTLE – NORMANDY, 1944

The office of Supreme Commander West was held by:
Field-Marshal von Rundstedt to July
Field-Marshal von Kluge to 18 August
Field-Marshal Model to 4 September

The Commander of Army Group B was:
Field-Marshal Rommel to 17 July
Field-Marshal von Kluge to 18 August
Field-Marshal Model to the end of the war

From the above, it can be seen that Field-Marshals von Kluge and Model both held simultaneously the posts of Supreme Commander West and Army Group B.

The Commander of the 7th Army was:
Colonel-General Dollmann to 28 June (died of a heart attack)
Obergruppenführer Hausser to 20 August
General Eberbach to 30 August

The Commander of Panzer Group West (which changed its name on 5 August to 5th Panzer Army) was:
General von Schweppenburg to 6 July
General Eberbach to 8 August
Obergruppenführer Dietrich

ORDER OF BATTLE PANZER GROUP WEST

1st SS, XLVII and XLVIII Panzer Corps; XXV, LXXIV, LXXXI, LXXXIV and LXXXVI Infantry Corps; II Airborne Corps

SS Oberstgruppenführer Paul Hausser (1880–1972) was one of the few officers who transferred from the Army into the SS and achieved high rank. He succeeded to the command of the 7th Army in Normandy in 1944, but was dismissed by Hitler in April 1945.

Appendix VII

Complete Order of Battle of the German Army, 12 April 1945

The order of battle on the following pages was that used during the final month of the Second World War, and was thus the one on which Hitler worked in the Berlin bunker.

It is important to realize that the divisions and corps shown on this order of battle were no longer at full strength, but were the burnt-out remnants of the formations which had been fighting for years.

Note also that in this order of battle, the corps were given Arabic numerals, not Roman ones.

Eastern Front

Army Group South

2nd Panzer Army
68th Corps: 71st Division; 13th SS Gebirgs Division (remnant only); 297th Division
22nd Gebirgs Corps: 118th Jäger Divisions; 9th SS Panzer Division
1st Cavalry Corps: 23rd Panzer Division; 4th Cavalry Division; 44th Division (battle group only); 3rd Cavalry Division; 14th SS Division; 16th SS Division

6th Army
18th Corps: 'Wolff' Battle Group (acting as 18 Corps)

4th SS Panzer Corps: 5th SS Division (battle group only); 3rd Panzer Division (battle group only); 1st Panzer Division (battle group only)
3rd Panzer Corps: 1st Volksgebirgs Division; 'Blocking Force' 'Motschmann'; 'Raithel' Battle Group
Army Reserve: 117th Jäger Division

6th Panzer Army (a.k.a. 6th SS Panzer Army)
1st SS Panzer Corps: 'Keitel' Battle Group; 356th Division (battle group only); 1st SS Panzer Division; 12th SS Panzer Division
'Schulz' Corps: 710th Division; 'Staudinger' Battle Group
2nd SS Panzer Corps: 'Folkmann' Battle Group; 'Von Buenau' Battle Group; 2nd SS Panzer Division; 3rd SS Panzer Division; 6th Panzer Division; 'Führer' Grenadier Division

8th Army
43rd Corps: 37th SS Cavalry Division; 96th Division; 101st Jäger Division (battle group only); 25th Panzer Division
'Feldherrenhalle' Panzer Corps: 357th Division; 1st and 2nd 'Feldherrenhalle' Divisions; 211th Volksgrenadier Division; 92nd Panzergrenadier Brigade
72nd Corps: 271st Volksgrenadier Division (battle group only); 46th Volksgrenadier Division; 711th Division (battle group only); 182nd Division

Army Reserve: SS Panzergrenadier Division 'Trabandt' (battle group only)

Army Group Reserve: From Army District 17, Fortress Area South-east; German GOC Slovakia; Fortress Brünn; 3rd Hungarian Division; 4th and 10th Para Divisions (being raised)

ARMY GROUP CENTRE

1st Panzer Army

9th Corps: 153rd Division; 15th Division; 8th Jäger Division (all battle groups); 76th Division

49th Gebirgs Corps: 320th Volksgrenadier Division; 'Baader' Division (battle group only); 304th Division (amalgamated with 16th Hungarian Division); 253rd Division; 3rd Gebirgs Division

59th Corps: 4th Gebirgs Division; 715th Division; 19th Panzer Division; 16th Panzer Division; 544th Volksgrenadier Division

11th Corps: 68th Division; 371st Division; 97th Jäger Division; 1st Skijäger Division; 158th Division

24th Panzer Corps: 10th Panzergrenadier Division; 78th Volks Assault Division; 254th Division; 344th Division

Army Reserve: 154th Division; 8th Panzer Division; 75th Division (being rested); 17th Panzer Division

Lieutenant-Colonel Weidinger, the steel-helmeted officer, taking part in the defence of Vienna, April 1945. The officer on the right, with his hands in his pockets, is General von Bunau, the battle commander in the Austrian capital.

17th Army

40th Panzer Corps: 168th Division; 20th Panzer Division: 45th Division

17th Corps: 31st SS Freiwilligen Grenadier Division; 269th Division (both only in battle group strength); 359th Division

Breslau Fortress: HQ 609th Division; Fortress Group 'Breslau'

8th Corps: 208th Division; 100th Jäger Division

Army Reserve: 1st Fallschirmpanzer Division 'Hermann Goering'; 20th SS Waffengrenadier Division (remnant); 603rd Division HQ; 18th SS Panzergrenadier Division (remnant)

4th Panzer Army

57th Panzer Corps: 6th Division; 72nd Division

Großdeutschland Panzer Corps: Panzergrenadier Division 'Brandenburg'; 615th Division HQ only; 545th Division (battle group only); Panzer Detachment 'Boehmen'

Moser's Corps Group: 193rd Division; 404th Division; 463rd Division

5th Corps: 344th Division; 36th SS Waffengrenadier Division (battle group only); 214th Division; 275th Division; 35th SS Polizei Division (battle group only)

Army Group Reserve: Oelmütz Fortress troops; 601st Division HQ; 602nd Division HQ; Führer Escort Division

OKH Reserve: 48th Panzer Corps; 21st Panzer Division; 10th SS Panzer Division

ARMY GROUP 'VISTULA'

9th Army

5th SS Gebirgs Corps: 391st Division HQ; 32nd SS Panzergrenadier Division; Division HQ Raegener (remnants 433 and 463 Divisions); detachments from Frankfurt Fortress

11th SS Corps: 702nd Division; 169th Division; 303rd Division; 20th Panzer-grenadier Division; 9th Para Division; Panzer Group 'Kurmark'

101st Corps: Infantry Division 'Großberlin'; 606th Division HQ; 5th Jäger Division

Army Reserve: 600th (Russian) Division; 56th Panzer Corps; 25th Panzergrenadier Division; Division 'Münchenberg'; 286th Training Division

3rd Panzer Army

46th Panzer Corps: 1st Naval Infantry Division; 547th Volksgrenadier Division

'Oder' Corps: 'Klosseck' Battle Group; 610th Division

32nd Corps: 281st Division; 'Stettin Fortress' Troops; 549th Volksgrenadier Division; 'Voigt' Battle Group

Swinemünde Defence Area: 3rd Naval Infantry Division; Navy Command 'Swinemünde'; 402nd Training Division

Army Reserve: 3rd SS Corps; 11th Panzergrenadier Division (being rested); 23rd SS Panzergrenadier Division (being rested); 28th Freiwilligen Grenadier Division (*en route*)

Army Group Reserve: Panzer Formation 'Baltic'; 156th Division (being rested); 227th Division HQ; 20th Luftwaffe Division; 541st Volksgrenadier Division (*en route*)

OKH Reserve: Army Group H (HQ and staff only); 4th Army Staff; 18th Panzergrenadier Division (being raised)

ARMY GROUP EAST PRUSSIA (FORMERLY 2ND ARMY)

Hela General Command

31st Volksgrenadier Division; 4th SS Polizeigrenadier Division; 7th Panzer Division; 203rd Division HQ; 83rd Division

23rd Corps

4th Panzer Division; 252nd Division; 12th Luftwaffe Field Division; 35th Division; 23rd Division; 32nd Division

18th Gebirgs Corps
7th Division

26th Corps
5th Panzer Division (amalgamated with remnants of 561st Volksgrenadier Division); 21st Division; 1st Division; 58th Division; 28th Jäger Division

9th Corps
93rd Division; 95th Division; 551st Volksgrenadier Division; Panzer Group from 'Großdeutschland' Corps; 14th Division

Commandant Pillau
50th Division; 558th Volksgrenadier Division; 286th Division; Naval Base (55th Corps) HQ only

6th Corps
129th Division; 170th Division

Army Reserve
HQ 349th Volksgrenadier Division; 61st Division (battle group only); 69th Division; 367th Division; 548th Volksgrenadier Division; 102nd Division (HQ only); 607th Division (HQ only); 10th Cyclist Jäger Brigade (HQ only)

OKH Reserve
27th Corps; 7th Corps; 542nd Volksgrenadier Division; 389th Division; 337th Volksgrenadier Division; 73rd Division; remnant Fallschirm/Panzer Corps 'Hermann Goering' (being rested); remnant 2nd 'Hermann Goering' Division (being rested); 28th Corps; 24th Panzer Division; 292nd Division; 131st Division; 56th Division; 562nd Volksgrenadier Division

ARMY GROUP KURLAND

18th Army
10th Corps: 121st Division; 30th Division
1st Corps: 132nd Division; 225th Division

2nd Corps: 87th Division; 263rd Division; 126th Division; 563rd Volksgrenadier Division
50th Corps: 290th Division; 11th Division
Army Reserve: Libau Fortress (HQ 52nd Security Division); 14th Panzer Division

16th Army
38th Panzer Corps: 329th Division; 122nd Division
6th SS Freiwilligen Corps: 19th Waffengrenadier SS Division; 24th Division; 12th Panzer Division
16th Corps: 218th Division plus Battle Group 'Barth'; HQ 21st Luftwaffe Field Division; 205th Division; 81st Division; 300th Division (HQ only)
Commander North Kurland: Coast Commandant (East Section); 207th Security Division HQ; Coast Commandants North and North West Sections; Fortress Commandant 'Windau', South West Section
Army Reserve: 'Kurland' Brigade
Army Group Reserve: 201st Security Division (HQ only); 15th Waffengrenadier SS Division (*en route*)

NORWAY

20TH GEBIRGS ARMY

19th Gebirgs Corps (Army Detachment 'Narvik')
6th Gebirgs Division; 388th Grenadier Brigade; 270th Division amalgamated with 193rd Grenadier Brigade

Corps Reserve
Bicycle Recce Brigade 'Norway'

71st Corps
503rd Grenadier Brigade; 140th Division; 139th Gebirgs Brigade; 210th Division amalgamated with Fortress Brigade 'Lofoten'; 230th Division

33rd Corps
14th Luftwaffe Field Division; 102nd Division; 295th Division

70th Corps
280th Division; 274th Division; 613th Division (HQ only)

36th Gebirgs Corps
Machine Gun Ski Brigade 'Finland'; Panzer Brigade 'Norway'

Army Reserve
7th Gebirgs Corps

DENMARK

Army Area 'Denmark'
160th Division; 233rd Division

Area Reserve
HQ 616th Division (North Jutland) (being raised)

SOUTH-WESTERN FRONT (ITALY)

ARMY GROUP C (SUPREME COMMANDER SOUTH-WEST)

Army of Liguria (also known as 87th Corps)
75th Corps: 5th Gebirgs Division; 2nd Italian Division (Littoria); 34th Division
'Lombardy' Corps: 3rd Italian Naval Division 'San Marco'; 134th Fortress Brigade; elements of 4th Italian Mountain Division 'Monte Rosa'
Reserve: Part of 4th Italian Mountain Division 'Monte Rosa'

14th Army
51st Gebirgs Corps: 148th Division; 1st Italian Division 'Italia'; 232nd Division; 114th Jäger Division; 334th Volksgrenadier Division
14th Panzer Corps: 94th Division; 8th Gebirgs Division; 65th Division

10th Army
1st Airborne Corps: 305th Division; 1st Para Division; 278th Volksgrenadier Division; 4th Para Division; 26th Panzer Division
76th Panzer Corps: 98th Volksgrenadier Division; 362nd Division; 42nd Jäger Division; 162nd (Turcoman) Division
73rd Corps: Alarm detachments only
Army Group Reserve: 155th Division (being rested); 90th Panzergrenadier Division; 29th Panzergrenadier Division

SOUTH-EASTERN FRONT (BALKANS)

ARMY GROUP E (SUPREME COMMANDER SOUTH-EAST)

97th Corps
188th Gebirgs Division; 237th Division

15th Gebirgs Corps
392nd (Croat) Division (remnant only); 104th Jäger Division

21st Gebirgs Corps
181st Division amalgamated with remnant of 369th (Croat) Division; mass of 7th SS Gebirgs Division; 969th Fortress Brigade; 966th Fortress Brigade; 964th Fortress Brigade; 1017th Fortress Brigade

34th Corps
Elements of 7th SS Gebirgs Division; 22nd Volksgrenadier Division; 41st Division; 963rd Fortress Brigade

91st Corps
11th Luftwaffe Field Division; 967th Fortress Brigade

15th Cossack Corps
1st and 2nd Cossack Divisions

69th Corps
'Fischer' Division (made up of 18th SS Police Gebirgs Regiment and 5th Police Regiment); 20th Reserve Jäger Regiment

Commandant East Aegean
939th Panzergrenadier Brigade (Rhodes); 968th Fortress Brigade

Commandant Crete
Fortress Division 'Crete'

Western Front

SUPREME COMMANDER NORTH WEST, HQ STAFF NORTH COAST

25th Army (Supreme Commander Netherlands)
617th Division (HQ only); 219th Division; 703rd Division
30th Corps: 249th Division; 20th Special Brigade HQ; 34th SS Grenadier Division 'Landstorm Nederland'
88th Corps: bulk of 346th Division; 361st Division; 6th Para Division; 169th Division

1st Airborne Army
2nd Para Corps: 8th Para Division; 7th Para Division, amalgamated with 346th Division; 245th Division (remnant only)
86th Corps: Panzer Group 'Großdeutschland'; 471st Division, amalgamated with remnant of 490th Division; 325th 'Fake' Division; 15th Panzergrenadier Division
Army Group Blumentritt
Corps HQ 'Ems' acting as 11th Corps: 480th Division; 172nd Special Services Division; 2nd Naval Infantry Division (battle group only); 3rd Panzergrenadier Division
Army Group B

Army Detachment von Luettwitz (47th Panzer Corps)
53rd Corps: Mass of 116th Panzer Division; 22nd Flak Division; 190th Division; 180th Division; 'Von Deichmann' Battle Group
58th Corps: 2nd Para Division; 'Hamburg' Infantry Division (HQ only)

15th Army
74th Corps: 272nd Volksgrenadier Division; bulk of 3rd Panzergrenadier Division; 'Meissner' Group; Panzer 'Lehr' Division; 338th Division; 176th Division
81st Corps: 106th Panzer Brigade; 'Wuertz' Battle Group; 'Scherzer' Battle Group
Army Group B Reserve: bulk of 326th Volksgrenadier Division; 340th Volksgrenadier Division; 5th Para Division; 166th Division
OKW Reserve: 41st Panzer Corps; 39th Panzer Corps (being rested)

SUPREME COMMANDER WEST

11th Army
66th Corps: Battle Group 116th Panzer Division; Battle Group 9th Panzer Division; SS Panzer Brigade 'Westfalen'; remnant of 277th Volksgrenadier Division
Acting as 9th Corps: battle groups from 326th and 26th Volksgrenadier Divisions
67th Corps: Battle Groups 'Großkreuz', 'Heidenreich', 'Ettner' and 'Feller'
Army Group G

7th Army
90th Corps: alarm detachments
85th Corps: 11th Panzer Division (remnant only); 'Schroetter Battle Group'
12th Corps (Army District 12): Battle Group 'von Berg'; 2nd Panzer Division
82nd Corps: 36th Volksgrenadier Division, amalgamated with remnant of 256th Volksgrenadier Division; 21st Flak Division; 416th Division
Army Reserve: 6th SS Gebirgs Division

1st Army

13th SS Corps: Panzer Brigade 'von Hube'; 'Bayern' Division; 79th Volksgrenadier Division; 212th Volksgrenadier Division; HQ 9th Volksgrenadier Division; 'Alpen' Infantry Division; HQ 616th Special Division

13th Corps: 553rd Volksgrenadier Division; 17th SS Panzergrenadier Division; 'Goetz von Berlichingen'; 246th Volksgrenadier Division; 19th Volksgrenadier Division; 2nd Gebirgs Division

19th Army

80th Corps: 559th Volksgrenadier Division; 198th Division; 47th Volksgrenadier Division; 16th Volksgrenadier Division

64th Corps: 716th Division; 257th Volksgrenadier Division; 106th Division

18th SS Corps: 405th Division; 805th Division; 1005th Brigade; Bauer's Brigade

Army Reserve: 189th Division (being raised)

Army Group G Reserve: 80th Corps; 352nd Volksgrenadier Division; 719th Division; 905th Special Division; 347th Volksgrenadier Division; 159th Division

Being raised or regrouped: 150th Division; 151st Division; 18th Volksgrenadier Division; 89th Division; 167th Division; 63rd Division; HQ 12th Army; HQ 24th Army; 'Weissenberger Group'; 407th Division HQ Staff; Staffs from Military Districts 6 and 7

OKW Reserve: being raised or rested: Infantry Division 'Theodor Koerner'; 3rd RAD; 38th SS Grenadier Division 'Nibelungen'; Panzer Division 'Clausewitz'

Struck off strength: 406th and 476th Divisions

Note. Naval forces in Lorient – a remnant of 265th Division – have been omitted from this order of battle.

INDEX

The Introduction and the Appendices are indexed as well as the main text. Page numbers in italic indicate illustrations.